THE COWGIRL COMPANION

BIG SKIES, BUCKAROOS, HONKY TONKS, LONESOME BLUES, AND OTHER GLORIES OF THE TRUE WEST

GAIL GILCHRIEST

HYPERION

NEW YORK

PERMISSIONS ACKNOWLEDGMENTS
PHOTO CREDITS APPEAR ON PAGE 179

"Be Yourself," by Georgie Connell Sicking. Previously published in *More Thinking*, Georgie Connell Sicking: Fallon, Nevada (1992). Reprinted by written permission of the author.

"Hey, Cowboy," by Peggy Godfrey. Previously published in *The Dry Crik Review*, Spring 1992. Reprinted by written permission of the author.

"Coming Home," by Laurie Wagner Buyer. Previously published in *The Dry Crik Review*, Winter 1992. Reprinted by written permission of the author.

"Cowgirling After Motherhood," by Kay Kelley. Previously published in *The Dry Crik Review*, Winter 1992. Reprinted by written permission of the author.

"Relapse," by Audrey Hankins. Previously published in *The Dry Crik Review*, Winter 1992. Reprinted by written permission of the author.

Obituary from Women's Pro Rodeo News, reprinted by written permission of the Women's Professional Rodeo Association, Blanchard, Oklahoma.

"Doctoring Worms," by Georgie Connell Sicking. Previously published in *Just Thinkin'*, Loganberry Press: Fallon, Nevada (1985). Reprinted by written permission of the author.

"Old Vogal," by Peggy Godfrey. Previously published in *The Dry Crik Review*, Winter 1992. Reprinted by written permission of the author.

"Thank Heavens for Dale Evans," by Martie Erwin, Robin Lynn Macy, and Lisa Brandenburg. As recorded by the Dixie Chicks on the LP *Thank Heavens for Dale Evans* (1990). Reprinted by written permission of the authors.

"Lead Mare," by Sue Wallis. Previously published in *The Exalted One*, Dry Crik Press: Lemon Cove, California (1991). Reprinted by written permission of the author.

"Girlfriends," by Sue Wallis. Previously published in *The Exalted One*, Dry Crik Press: Lemon Cove, California (1991). Reprinted by written permission of the author.

Library of Congress Cataloging-in-Publication Data

Gilchriest, Gail
    The cowgirl companion : big skies, buckaroos, honky tonks, lonesome blues, and other glories of the true West / Gail Gilchriest. — 1st ed.
        p.   cm.
    ISBN 1–56282–868–1
    1. Cowgirls—West (U.S.) 2. West (U.S.)—Social life and customs. 3. West (U.S.)—Popular culture—History. I. Title
F596.G55 1993
978'.0082—dc20   92-29953
                                                      CIP

Design/production by Robert Bull Design

FIRST EDITION

10 9 8 7 6 5 4 3 2 1

ACKNOWLEDGMENTS

WHEN I FIRST started this project, Amarillo cowgirl Cindy Price let me tag along while she mended a fence. In the pasture, an enormous bull eyed us ominously. Cindy strode right up to this ton or two of irritable beef and slapped his rear. Then she turned to me—her lower lip packed with snuff—and said, "Watch out for this one, he'll run over ya."

I took her at her word. Terrified, I stood behind the truck. Embarrassed by my cowardice, I pretended that I had lost an earring and was searching for it beneath the safety of the big Chevy.

I'll admit I was terrified by livestock when I started this project. And I was in awe of cowgirls. I still get a funny feeling in my stomach whenever I'm in bovine company, and the pedestal upon which I place cowgirls towers even higher than before.

Special thanks to all the cowgirls and cowboys—both literal and spiritual—without whom this wouldn't have been possible:

Geri Thoma, Robin Macy, the Dixie Chicks, Cynthia Kinney, Karla Roberson Puckett, Lucy Herring, Dale Evans Rogers, Roy Rogers, Jr., Blair and Julie Bresnan, the National Cowgirl Hall of Fame, Lydia Moore and the Women's Professional Rodeo Association, the National Little Britches Rodeo Association, John Gilman and Robert Heide, Ken Brown, Anna Lively, Susan Paisley, the Buffalo Bill Historical Center, the King Ranch Archives, Alicia Neuhaus, Linda and Les Davis, Virginia and Chope Phillips, Fern

ACKNOWLEDGMENTS

Sawyer, Cindy Price, Rebecca and Richard and Reba Gonzales, Jeanna Clare, Patsy Montana, Susan Jackson of Deep Texas, the Western Folklife Center, Nancy Kelley Sheppard, Sherry Delamarter and the Cowgirl Hall of Fame Barbecue, Guadalupe Hand Prints, Cathy Boswell, Betty Goodan Andrews, Lea Sage, Sonna Warvel, Lynn "Jonnie" Jonckowski, Shalah Perkins, Joyce Gibson Roach, Vana Beissinger, Angie Meadors, the Professional Rodeo Cowboys Association, Marilyn Weber, Ronda Harrison, Michael Casella, Betsy Matheson, Jim Sargent, Georgie Connell Sicking, Peggy Godfrey, Laurie Wagner Boyer, Kay Kelley, Audrey Hankins, Lisa Brandenburg, Sue Wallis, Christine Archibald, David Thompson, Jackie Golden, Sophie Sartain, Chrissy Armstrong, Brook and LaNita Gilchriest, Shirley Gilchriest, and Jim Reeder, Jr.

CONTENTS

INTRODUCTION

I NEVER INTENDED to become a cowgirl. Sure, I grew up on a ranch, and I loved riding horses when I was a child. I knew my way around a milk cow all right, but never, ever did I dream cowgirl dreams. "Cowgirl" just wasn't a career option back then, at least not a very glamorous one. Movie star—that's what little girls of my generation longed to be.

I didn't exactly go straight from the farm to the big screen at the Bijou, however. For years I typed and answered the phone in an insurance office, singing on the radio at night and on weekends and in my spare time. "Happy Trails to You" wasn't part of my repertoire in those days. There was no fringe in my wardrobe, no cowboy boots. And Roy Rogers? Well, he was simply a famous cowboy I'd seen in the movies, not someone I personally knew. After many years in radio, Fate led me to Hollywood, where I more or less stumbled into the role of Queen of the West.

During my first days in movieland, my agent presented me to producers as the singing-sophisticate type. Back then, any actress depending on work in westerns to keep food on her table grew thin. Cowboys like Gene Autry and Hopalong Cassidy and Roy Rogers were kings of Saturday-morning cinema. A woman playing opposite a cowboy star could count herself lucky if she got third billing behind the cowboy and his horse.

My movie career as a "glamour girl" didn't grind to a halt, but it didn't exactly set the world afire either. Then I landed a part in *The Cowboy and the Señorita* with Roy Rogers, and the fan mail came pouring in. I figured I could do a lot worse than riding a horse and occasionally saying, "He went thataway!" So I kept my boots on, and made more westerns. I enjoyed riding. I liked working outdoors, and I established such a rapport with my co-star that I later married him.

The cowgirl role fit me just fine, on screen and off. Roy and I raised our family on a ranch. Even though Hollywood can sometimes warp personal perspective, we always tried to teach our children the importance of cowgirl/cowboy values—courage, compassion, family, and faith.

Over the years I've discovered that there's more to being a cowgirl than punching cows, or winning rodeo trophies, or galloping off into a movie sunset with Roy. Cowgirl is an attitude, really. A pioneer spirit, a special American brand of courage. The cowgirl faces life head on, lives by her own lights, and makes no excuses. Cowgirls take stands. They speak up. They defend the things they hold dear. A cowgirl might be a rancher, or a barrel racer, or a bull rider, or an actress. But she's just as likely to be a checker at the local Winn Dixie, a full-time mother, a banker, an attorney, an astronaut.

Children of my generation longed to be movie stars. Today, even movie stars want to be cowgirls. I'm in my golden years, as they say, but I still sometimes find myself thinking about what I'd like to be when I grow up. It's sort of silly, I know, but—I think I'd like to be a cowgirl.

—Dale Evans Rogers
Los Angeles, August 1992

THE COWGIRL COMPANION

BIG SKIES, BUCKAROOS, HONKY TONKS, LONESOME BLUES, AND OTHER GLORIES OF THE TRUE WEST

CHAPTER ONE

GO WEST, YOUNG WOMAN

WILL ROGERS supposedly said it first. One afternoon long before he came to international fame with pithy one-liners, such as "I never met a man I didn't like," Rogers dropped by the Oklahoma ranch of his friend Zack Mulhall. There the cowboy philosopher witnessed an amazing sight: Mulhall's daughter, Lucille, roping and riding alongside the other ranch hands—and outroping and outriding most of the men.

Even wearing a skirt, thirteen-year-old Lucille appeared one with her horse, cutting cows from the herd with surgically precise turns. At a gallop, she swung an almost liquid lasso, launching clean loops through the air to

COW GIRL.
WITH BUFFALO BILL'S
WILD WEST

snag her wild-eyed targets. Story goes that little Lucille could rope anything and wrestle it to the ground.

And so Will Rogers watched this spectacle. Maybe he took off his Stetson, scratched his head, and pondered the scene for a moment or two, eating the dust kicked up by the activity of Zack Mulhall's unconventional daughter. When he finally spoke, witty Will reportedly welded the words "cow" and "girl" to create a single descriptive noun. It was 1899, and the label may have been new, but the concept was not.

Cowgirl, the obvious feminine of cowboy, was hardly an ingenious coinage—not Rogers at his pearly best with the language to be sure.

Lucille Mulhall
—aka "The Lassoer in Lingerie"
—inspired the coinage
of the word "cowgirl."

But then again maybe it wasn't Will Rogers doing the innovating anyhow. Another perfectly nice version of the same story has Theodore Roosevelt forming the compound "cowgirl" when dazzled by the macho maneuvers of dainty Lucille. More than likely neither Rogers nor Roosevelt was the very first human to speak the word. And Lucille Mulhall certainly wasn't the first female to do the work.

Cowgirling started long before Lucille ever threw a loop, probably sometime in the early 1800s, when thousands of men, women, and children joined wagon trains departing the cities of the East for the greener pastures of the trans-Mississippi wilderness. In a way, the conception of the American cowgirl occurred at the precise moment that first wagon lurched forward, creaking toward the sunset. At that time the vast frontier would scarcely have supported a single sewing circle. Plenty of Native Americans, scads of buffalo, a few white men—mostly hunters, fugitives, and vaqueros—dotted the plains, but prior to the first shouts of "Wagons, ho!" white women remained mostly creatures of the civilized East.

Almost from the beginning of the overland migration, however, women roped, rode, and drove cattle across the plains. Not many women, mind you, but a brave—or crazy—few. Widows, ranchers' wives and daughters, even a few gutsy bachelorettes saddled up and bucked convention. Wearing spurs and bran-

828-B, LUCILLE MULHALL WORLDS CHA

dishing lassos, these gals weren't about to leave all the adventure of the West to the men.

The cowgirl didn't just pop up out of the prairie like a wildflower. Instead, she evolved gradually out of the western experience.

First, there was the pioneer woman, the Prairie Madonna. You know the type, sunbonneted matrons like Ma Ingalls from *Little House on the Prairie*. Or maybe you recognize her from western art—wearing a long skirt and gripping a rifle, her frightened children huddled behind her. The Prairie Madonna went West reluctantly. She braved hunger, disease, wicked weather, harsh environment, and the loneliness of frontier life in a dutiful, stand-by-your-man sort of way. And while she didn't always embrace life on the frontier, she did rise to meet its challenges.

Not too surprisingly, a few pioneer women discovered that sitting tall in the saddle under the big western sky beat the hell out of housework. And the housewives who preferred branding cattle to baking cornbread—those gals whose hearts beat a little faster at roundup

YOU'D BETTER SMILE WHEN YOU CALL ME THAT

In the days of the Old West, a woman couldn't rightly call herself a cowgirl unless her friends and enemies called her something else. Among the more colorful nicknames:

- Kitty the Schemer
- Airship Annie
- China Mary
- Altershanks Eva
- Bowlegged Mary
- Faro Nell
- One-Eyed Slim
- Bronco Sue
- Cattle Kate
- Cheese-Head Hanna

- The Bandit Queen
- Duchess of Winchester
- Madame Moustache
- Little Britches
- Little Big Hair
- Little Sure Shot
- Poker Alice
- Rose of Cimarron

- Calamity Jane
- Leadville Lil
- Unsinkable Molly
- Sidesaddle Sal
- Slow-Witted Wilma
- Freckle-Faced Fran
- The Lassoer in Lingerie
- Lispin' Lilly
- Javelina Hattie
- Pinky

time—represented the second step toward cowgirls becoming a fully developed character in the Old West tableau.

Right along with horsewomanship came markswomanship. Life was rough on the range, and neophyte cowgirls learned to sling guns on both sides of the law. Lady outlaws—desperadas, horse thieves,

rustlers—weren't cowgirls in the strictest sense, but they contributed to the overall cowgirl persona.

And then there was Lucille. During a period when a woman wearing trousers caused heads to swivel, and a lady dragging on a cigarette drew gasps of disapproval, the antics of Lucille Mulhall created quite a stir. The daughter of an affluent rancher/railroad executive/showman, Lucille qualified as a sure-enough western prodigy, riding at age two and sticking like a postage stamp to the back of any horse she mounted by the time she turned eight. Before she reached her twelfth birthday, she could lasso a running jackrabbit, rope a full-grown steer, and use her reata to catch the hind legs of a racing calf—a trick so difficult that many men gave up on it, aiming for the calf's neck instead.

When her father once jokingly told Lucille she could keep any cows she roped and branded by herself, the little girl quickly amassed a nice-sized herd of her own. Theodore Roosevelt, a dinner guest at the Mulhalls' ranch one evening, bet young Lucille an invitation to his inaugural celebration that she couldn't rope a wolf. The Bull Moose lost the wager.

The Mulhalls were such a cow-oriented family that they even called one of their daughters "Bossy." At the ranch they hosted English-style fox hunts, complete with hounds and trumpets and pink riding jackets. But in Oklahoma, with few foxes, the Mulhalls chased wolves. Visitors to the Mulhall spread left so impressed by the cowboying youngsters that Colonel Mulhall organized a touring Wild West act around Lucille and his other three children. In addition to performing at local rodeos and cowboy contests, the family played the St. Louis World's Fair in 1904. Will Rogers was part of the Mulhall troupe, as was future movie star Tom Mix. But Lucille always pulled star billing. In 1905, throngs of adoring fans trailed Lucille and her pretty sisters wherever they went in New York City. The first time she roped in public there, the disbelieving audience mobbed her and tore at her clothing to see if she was really a man.

And so, around the turn of the century, "Lucille fever" swept the nation. "Cowgirl" seemed a fairly straightforward description when compared with some of the other silly-sounding monikers news-

THE COWGIRL POET

Be Yourself

By Georgie Connell Sicking

When I was young and foolish
the women said to me
Take off those spurs and comb
your hair, if a lady you would be.

Forget about them cowboy ways
come and sit awhile
We will try to clue you in on women's
ways and wiles.

Take off that Levi jumper, put up
those batwing chaps
Put on a little makeup and we can get a
date for you "perhaps."

Forget about that ropin'—that will make
calluses on your hands
And you know it takes soft fingers
if you want to catch a man.

Do away with that Stetson hat for it
will crush your curls
And even a homely cowboy wouldn't
date a straight-haired girl.

Now bein' young and foolish I went
my merry way
And I guess I never wore a dress
until my wedding day.

Now I tell my children, no
matter what you do
stand up straight and tall,
be you and only you.

For if the lord had meant us
all to be alike
And the same rules to keep
He would have bonded us together,
just like a
flock of sheep.

papermen penned when writing about Lucille—dubbing her The Queen of the Range, the Female Conqueror of Beef and Horn, the Lassoer in Lingerie, the Cowboy Cowgirl.

Lucille and other daring women of the Wild West shows, the fearless broncobusting queens of the rodeo, the darlings in dime novels, and ultimately the wholesome, perfectly coiffed buckaroos of the movies galvanized America's picture of the cowgirl. The cowgirl stepped into the limelight as the ultimate female individualist, the quintessential all-American heroine, the embodiment of star-spangled womanly courage. Blazing her own trail, living according to her own lights, the cowgirl trampled over anyone who attempted to trim her wings or squeeze her into a corset. The iconoclast became an icon.

The early cowgirl cowgirled quietly. Wearing trousers, braving the wilds, or working alongside men and animals was not considered ladylike conduct for the Victorian age. While the cowboy emerged as a near-mythic character of folk legend, living loudly, boasting and swaggering and chivalrously tipping his ten-gallon to ladies on the streets of Cheyenne, the cowgirl kept a low profile, shoving her long curls up under her Stetson and trying not to draw attention to her myriad infractions of society's rules.

While widely held notions about femininity often impeded a girl's cowboyish ambitions, it did not keep all women out of the corral; a few wily would-be cattlewomen discovered that becoming a boy made a fine first step toward becoming a cowboy.

An Idaho woman conveniently named Jo Monaghan lived most of her life disguised as a man. She had a reputation as a skilled horse handler, broncobuster and all-around dependable hand with livestock. But, standing only five feet in boots, Jo didn't show the customary cowboy zeal for gambling or boozing or whoring. As a result, people thought "him" a peculiar fellow.

If Jo's calling hadn't been cattle, she might have made it on the stage. Like Yul Brynner in the role of the King of Siam, Jo Monaghan found a part that fit just fine and then stuck to it till the end. After many years in the saddle and an almost flawless performance as cowboy, her true identity came to light only at her death.

Ranching the open range wasn't the easiest way for a gal to make a living. To use an analogy popularized by current Texas Governor Ann Richards, the cowgirl's role in settling the West was much like that of dancer Ginger Rogers in the movies: She did all the fancy footwork Fred Astaire did, except backward and in high heels. The early cowgirl tackled all the tasks the cowboy undertook—except she did it wearing a skirt and with a baby at her breast.

In a sense, the cowgirl "had it all" long before female partners in two-income marriages started trying to juggle career, housework, and motherhood. A century before telemarketing or Tupperware, farming and cattle ranching were quite possibly the original stay-at-home careers. Many ranch women kept house, raised children, and still rode with the herd.

Mary Ann "Molly" Goodnight is remembered as the ultimate, early-day homemaker on the range. She often accompanied her husband, Colonel Charles Goodnight, and his cowboys on drives, handling a wagon, cooking, and doctoring animals as well as men. At home she raised baby buffalo as a hobby, entertained lavishly, and later became a well-known philanthropist in the Texas panhandle.

Not all women approached ranch life with such grace. About the same time Molly Goodnight strived to make her husband's life in rough territory more civilized, Lizzie Johnson made her man's existence a cattleman's hell. At various times a teacher, part-time bookkeeper and writer, Lizzie didn't see cowpunching as a sideline to her wifely duties; she put her career up front from the start.

Lizzie was one of the first women to register her own brand. She and her husband, Hezekiah, drove cattle up the trail together in the 1870s and 1880s. Well, sort of together: she drove her herd and he drove his. A shrewd businesswoman, Lizzie demanded that Hezekiah sign a prenuptial agreement stating that all her property would remain hers and hers alone, along with any profits she made during the course of the marriage. Rumor has it that Lizzie, much more astute than Hezekiah in money matters, was even known to tattoo her husband's unmarked stock with her brand. In fact, the only way Lizzie attempted to make her mate's life easier was to let him ride in her wagon every now and then. Hezekiah eventually left Lizzie a widow.

Many a woman's cattle career began at the funeral parlor, and other times a rancher's death left a daughter in charge. Very occasionally a woman would embark on a cattle endeavor alone from the beginning. There is legend of an all-girl ranching enterprise in central Texas in the 1880s.

A few early cowgirls brandished guns with the daring and verve most women reserved for the darning needle. Molly Owens of Arizona, for one, kept her handgun hidden in a special pocket of her apron, because in the Wild West a woman never knew when she'd be called from her cooking to kill an Indian, a rustler, or any other of a wide variety of scoundrels.

A south Texas woman bossing her own cattle operation reputedly blew a man's head off for getting fresh with her. Another fellow flirted a bit too much with a New Mexico gal known as Lady Castille. Not in the mood for his friskiness, she asked him to leave. He refused. So she pulled her pistol and whizzed a bullet right past his ear. Then she said, "I didn't try to hit you that time, I just wanted to show you I mean what I say."

Texan Sally Skull didn't wait for widowhood to make her a cattle baroness—she got divorced, then went about swinging pistols spewing obscenities, and putting her Circle S brand on most anything that moved. If today's heavily armed urban outlaws are said to "pack heat," Sally toted her day's equivalent of a thermonuclear arsenal. In addition to a rifle, a couple of pistols, and a bouquet of knives, Sally also wielded a whip, with which she could pop bluebonnets right off their stems.

Sally plied her trade along the Rio Grande, dealing horses on both sides of the border. Realizing hers was not a wholesome environment for children, she sent her two young ones away to school.

Things became tense between Sally and her daughter following an incident in New Orleans when Sally visited the child at school. The daughter's beloved little dog tried to bite Sally, so she drew her pistol and sent the pooch to his final doggie reward. It seems Sally's bite was worse than her bark.

Firearms enthusiasts often quip, "God created all men, Sam Colt made them equal." This folksy dictum carried weight with women on the frontier, where a gun lent a gal a certain confidence—if she knew how to use it. Not all women relied on Colts and Winchesters to defend themselves. Lola Montez, an early-day stage performer in California, was known for her efficacy with a riding crop. She reportedly lashed her lovers with it from time to time. Mrs. Grace Newton's weapon of choice was language. A judge presiding over Mrs. Newton's trial on charges of cattle rustling adjourned the court simply as a result of the defendant's foul mouth. The magistrate said the recess would last "until such time as she can testify like a lady."

Even though they wore pants, punched cattle, carried guns, and sometimes scalded the hide off horses with their salty language, most early cowgirls did not seek fame or notoriety. Gun-wielding female outlaws, however, seemed to bask (and occasionally fry) in the limelight. Desperadas like Belle Starr and Calamity Jane probably wouldn't have called themselves cowgirls, but they still represent an important thread in the fabric of western lore.

Belle Starr, the glamorous Bandit Queen, was called harridan by some, heroine by others. Most people agree that Belle registered closer to sinner than saint on the virtue spectrum, but even now, a full century after her murder, Belle has her admirers. Her grave and cabin in Porum, Oklahoma, still attract tourists. Some writers have described her as beautiful and glamorous, comparing her to Joan of Arc, Venus, and Cleopatra. Others paint her as an ugly, crude, immoral nymphomaniac.

Born Myra Belle Shirley, the daughter of Missouri innkeepers, Belle attended private school as a girl, learning Greek, Latin, arithmetic, spelling, and other standard subjects of the day. As a teenager, she fell in with a group of bad boys. Call it a vice: the woman had a fatal attraction for scamps, thieves, and killers.

WALK LIKE A MAN, ACT LIKE A LADY

Etiquette for the Modern Cowgirl

- Leave muddy boots outside the door of the trailer.
- Beer and whiskey, mighty risky.
- Always look your best at church.
- Always look your *very* best at the rodeo.
- Don't go looking for a fight.
- Don't walk away from a fight.
- Don't dip snuff indoors.
- Thou shalt not covet thy neighbor's husband.
- No spitting at the VFW.
- No heavy petting—right at first.
- No cussing in front of children.
- No white boots before Easter.
- No straw hats after Labor Day.
- No such thing as hair *too* big.
- No such thing as eye shadow *too* blue.
- No such thing as Wranglers *too* tight.
- No snickering during castration time.
- Flush with your foot.

Cordially yours,
Jacqueline White

Jesse James befriended Belle when she was young, as did fellow thug Cole Younger. In her never-ending search for the love of a bad man, Belle married three times, always to a fellow living on the fringes of or way outside the law. As her friends and husbands robbed stages, filched livestock, and committed homicides, Belle kept up appearances. She played piano briefly in a Dallas dance hall. She ran a livery stable, cultivated respectable friends, dressed elegantly, and conducted herself like a lady—sometimes.

In her law-abiding moments Belle rode sidesaddle. When in a mischievous mood she went about disguised as a man, and probably took part in several of her gang's nefarious capers. Belle was never personally proven guilty of murder. However, she did for a fact aid and abet criminals, and a horse theft conviction once earned her a nine-month stay in the local hoosegow. Perhaps a little of Belle's appeal had something to do with the dichotomy of her lifestyle. Was she a lady or a tramp? Or both?

No such contradiction cut the life of Martha Jane Cannary, better known as Calamity Jane. She dressed as a man most of her life, and earned her nickname by crowing that awful calamity would befall any rascal who opposed her. Calamity's early career consisted mostly of drifting around the West on a succession of drinking binges, each of which she euphemistically called a "high lonesome." Boozing, disturbing the peace, and disseminating her own legend filled Calamity's days. She claimed to have been a scout for General Custer, although records don't confirm the story. And she bragged of a romance with gunfighter James B. "Wild Bill" Hickok. Some of her biographers assert that Calamity and Wild Bill were indeed briefly married, but others suggest that the Wild Bill love story was probably wild bull—more of Calamity's boastful noise. She was, however, kind-hearted, and when she was sober, which was seldom, she had a reputation as a solicitous, selfless nurse to smallpox sufferers. In her later years, Calamity portrayed herself in Wild West shows. More ne'er-do-well than bad girl, Calamity Jane's special knack wasn't for crime, but instead for simultaneous self-destruction and self-promotion.

Then there were the lady rustlers, the shoplifters of the open range. Annie McDoulet, or "Cattle Annie," and her sidekick Jennie "Little Britches" Stevens, a couple of sticky-lassoed teenagers, rode with the Doolin Gang in 1894. They purloined ponies and cows, and sometimes sold whiskey to Native Americans for a little extra pocket money. Rose Dunn, known as "Rose of Cimarron," rustled with the Doolin Gang, too.

Ella Watson of Kansas hated housework so much she high-tailed it to Wyoming and started collecting cows illegally. They called Ella "Cattle Kate" because of her reputation for "finding" cattle, or referred to her as the "Duchess of Winchester" owing to her acumen with a rifle. By some accounts Cattle Kate stole steers, plain and simple; other history buffs theorize she was more of a fence, accepting hot cattle from cowboys in exchange for sexual favors. Her guilt has never been proven, but neither has her innocence. Whether upstanding citizen, cow burglar, or middleman madam, Cattle Kate ultimately swung from a pine tree, lynched along with her partner in crime by fed-up neighboring cattlemen.

Americans in the early years of the century were as fascinated by the West as Americans today are by outer space. During the days just after the settling of the frontier, even the president—Teddy Roosevelt, a Harvard-educated Manhattanite—ranched in Dakota Territory, affecting a cowboy persona and embracing the Old West

PONY TALES

Acowgirl loves her cows, but she can't go crying after every old moo-girl leaving the ranch on a stock car. Horses, however; there's another story. See a cowgirl with the blues, and ten-to-one says her best horse has headed on to Greener Pastures.

"Why this horse right here can stop on a dime and give ten cents change." Listen to a ranch gal talk about her favorite pony for a few minutes—or a few hours—and you'll wonder why she's called cowgirl and not "horsegirl."

Every cowgirl believes hers to be the smartest horse in the universe. One woman, strapping on some odd but colorful braggadocio, insisted that her number-one mount had two pretty colors, "palomino and fat." Lucille Mulhall billed her hoofed friend Governor as the "$10,000 Wonder Horse." People bought tickets for the privilege of seeing Governor walk on his knees.

Women's Pro Rodeo News runs an obituary when a famous horse dies. And why not? Rodeo star Charmayne James Rodman thinks of her horse Scamper as a business partner; together they earn a rather cushy income racing barrels on the professional circuit. To hear a cowgirl tell it, a good horse, her horse, can do anything short of counting cattle.

Hollywood cowgirl Dale Evans boasts that her saddled pal Buttermilk instinctively knew to start performing whenever he heard the buzzer indicating that the movie cameras had begun to roll. "He knew my cheap tricks," Dale says, "and I knew his." So great, in fact, was Dale's affection for Buttermilk that she and Roy had him stuffed and mounted by a taxidermist after his death. Today Buttermilk stands, an equine mannequin, alongside Roy's Trigger, "The Smartest Horse in the Movies," at the Roy Rogers and Dale Evans Museum in Victorville, California.

It's been said that ranching is hell on horses and women. Perhaps that's why working cowgirls bond so emotionally with their mounts.

Fanny Sperry Steele, a famous early-day rodeo rider, summed it up this way, "If horses aren't in heaven, I don't want to go there."

milieu. Just as little boys of the 1960s wanted to become astronauts, boys of the early 1900s dreamed cowboy dreams. And in the same way Sally Ride opened the door for women to aspire to space exploration, the cowgirls of Wild West shows and rodeos at the turn of the century let girls embrace hopes of cowboy adventure too.

Audiences hungered for anything western, and around 1883 Wild West shows began touring the country. Part rodeo, part county fair, part vaudeville revue, the Wild West shows were sort of specialty circuses with a western theme. The program typically included impressive demonstrations of roping and riding and shooting along with a simulated pony express ride, a staged buffalo hunt, a melodramatic enactment of an Indian attack on a frontier settlement, plus assorted depictions of Native American customs. "Step right up," ringmasters like the famous Indian fighter William F. "Buffalo Bill" Cody implored, "and see the curious creatures of the West: the Indian, the buffalo, and the women in trousers riding wild horses and shooting guns."

Buffalo Bill devised the first widely watched Wild West show, and Annie Oakley emerged as his first big star. The most famous pistol-packing mama in the history of the West qualified as neither cowgirl nor outlaw. She was an entertainer. Deadeye gunwoman Phoebe Ann Moses changed her name to Annie Oakley for no apparent reason. She learned to shoot at age eight, and helped support her family by supplying game to a nearby hotel. At age fifteen she defeated champion marksman Frank Butler, and later married him.

Annie Oakley's awe-inspiring gunslinging involved tricks such as shooting a coin from her husband's hand and nailing a playing card with a bullet from ninety feet away. Once she even blasted a cigarette from the mouth of German Crown Prince Wilhelm without so much as grazing the royal lip. "Little Sure-Shot," the famous Sioux chief Sitting Bull christened her—"Little" because she stood only five feet tall, and "Sure Shot"—well, with a weapon in hand, diminutive Annie towered above any man. She knew nothing of cows, cowboys, riding, or roping, and when she joined Buffalo Bill's Wild West Show in 1885, Annie Oakley had never ventured west of Cincinnati. Even before Will Rogers called little Lucille Mulhall a cowgirl, Annie

Oakley had blasted the western woman's way off the plains and onto the stages, stadiums, and front pages of the world.

Along with the rising popularity of the Wild West show rode rodeo. Less theatrical but no less dramatic exhibitions of cowboy skill, early rodeos featured bronc riding, steer bulldogging, bull riding, and wild-horse racing.

At first, many of the stars featured in Wild West shows and rodeos were actual ranchers, real-life cowboys and cowgirls taking time out from their chores to dazzle a crowd. But increasingly the performers were just that: performers, full-time entertainers who found show business more lucrative than beef business.

Barbara "Tad" Lucas, the late rodeo star from Fort Worth,

COOL COWGIRLS

It's Not Just a Job—It's a Spirit

- Dale Evans
- Ava Gardner
- Thelma and Louise
- Aretha Franklin
- Faye Wattleton
- Whoopi Goldberg
- Penny Marshall
- Madonna
- Susan Sarandon
- Georgia O'Keeffe
- Linda Barry
- Oprah Winfrey
- Gloria Steinem
- Charmayne Rodman
- Catwoman
- Anita Hill
- The women of the All-American Girls' Professional Baseball League
- Murphy Brown
- Amelia Earhart
- Jodie Foster
- Patsy Montana
- Hillary Clinton
- The Designing Women
- Sandra Day O'Connor
- Sally Ride

exemplified the trend. Like most of the early Wild Westers and rodeo hands, Tad hailed from a ranching background. The youngest of twenty-four children, she cut her cowgirling teeth on her parent's spread in Nebraska. At age thirteen Tad rode wild cows at a gathering of local ranchers. Soon afterward she found work as a jockey, and in 1918 she earned the then royal sum of $25 for staying atop a wicked steer at a community fair. It didn't take a sharp gal like Tad too long to discover that good horse sense mixed with a touch of showmanship could combine for an exciting lifestyle. In an exhibition at Madison Square Garden in 1923 she boarded bucking Brahmans (pronounced BRAY-mers by cowgirls). The next year she wowed audiences with a show of trick riding at Wembley Stadium in London, ultimately going on to slamdunk several All-Around Cowgirl Championships and assorted trick-riding titles in Chicago, New York, and Sydney, Australia. By the dawn of the Jazz Age, Tad Lucas was one of a handful of women who'd emerged as western-style "flappers" of sorts; gracefully flapping around on the backs of wild livestock and earning big money doing it.

Soon after Tad and other cowgirls wandered off the range and onto the stage in cities all over the U.S. and Europe, a faint dividing line began to appear between Wild West performer and female ranch hand. The true cowpoke ultimately eschewed the high-life, preferring instead the hard work and solitude of cattle tending. The more show-business-oriented cowgirl glossed her machismo with a veneer of glamour and daintiness. This seemingly contradictory combination of masculine bravery and feminine sex appeal thrilled audiences. And once the cowgirl started sewing sequins on her chaps, it was just a short trot from the rodeo arena to the silver screen.

If Wild West shows and rodeos brought cowgirl heroics to every town in America, pulp fiction brought them to every lap. At first cowboys, and later, to a lesser extent, cowgirls, saved the day in the widely read action adventure stories published in periodicals such as *Rough Rider Weekly* and in cliff-hanging dime novels with melodramatic titles such as *The Detective Queen; or, The Denver Doll's Devices*, and *King of the Wild West's Nerve; or, Stella in the Saddle*.

Before about 1906 the western heroines of popular fiction tended mostly to be genteel, helpless creatures sprinkled into a story simply for the hero to rescue. But with the advent of more active fictional women with colorful names like Hurricane Nell, Rowdy Kate, and Leadville Lil, the traditional roles were sometimes temporarily reversed, allowing the cowgirl to save the cowboy from doom.

Although the women of these sorts of stories did eventually become more than mealy-mouthed swooners waiting to be snatched from the jaws of death by the courageous cowboy, the cowgirl heroine seldom, if ever, got the man at the story's end. America embraced the romantic notion of a woman on a bronco, a woman marksman. They

Bucking convention
—pioneer rodeo cowgirls
of the 1920s.

gobbled up the female cowboy, no questions asked; but post-Victorian audiences weren't quite ready for the cowgirl with a libido. While the cowboy of the pulp fiction sowed his wild oats, the cowgirl talked to her horse.

Once Wild West shows, rodeos, and dime novels had paved the way, the cinema took the cowboy and cowgirl to new entertainment horizons. The action of dime novels fit perfectly into the short two-reel serial format popular with early filmmakers and moviegoers. Between 1910 and 1920 these shorts as well as a few feature-length films presented former rodeo performer Helen Gibson (wife of cowboy star Hoot Gibson), a glamorous gal dubbed Texas Guinan, and others in what were essentially dime novels for the screen.

Good stomping the daylights out of Evil just in the nick of time. In the years following World War I, audiences young and old couldn't get enough of these simple, reassuring storylines. The popularity of westerns continued after World War II. Americans felt invincible and heady after the dramatic hard-fought victory over Europe and Japan, and movie moguls capitalized on this euphoria. Studio executives found the "horse opera" or western to be the perfect vehicle for these feel-good morality plays. The winning formula: Every Saturday morning pack hundreds of children into local movie houses and run a couple of reels of Roy Rogers foiling the mortgage-foreclosing banker, rounding up rascally rustlers, lending a hand to imperiled women, and finally riding off into the sunset singing a sweet cowboy song.

As real cowboys raised beef in anonymity back on the ranch, the reel cowboys of Hollywood generated box-office receipts and more. Merchandisers mined gold with cowboy tie-ins. Little Billy went cowboy loco, little Suzie too. Boys and girls begged parents for a Hopalong Cassidy bicycle, a Gene Autry lunch box, or even a Tom Mix Golden Plastic Bullet Telescope.

The female lead in most western movies added up to little more than a supporting role. Cowboys were movie stars; cowgirls were scenery. If an actress in a western received third billing in a film, behind the cowboy and his horse, she could count herself lucky. While Hollywood produced all sorts of major cowboy stars, from Gary Cooper to John Wayne to Clint Eastwood, the high-magnitude cowgirl star never rose—even though eventually, with Elizabeth Taylor in *Giant*, Jane Russell in *The Outlaw*, and Marilyn Monroe in *The Misfits*, celluloid cowgirls were permitted to add "sexy" to the long laundry list of desirable all-American attributes they possessed.

If any actress approached stardom as a cowgirl, it was Dale Evans, the fresh-faced girl pardner of Roy Rogers. At first she trotted alongside the King of the Cowboys in films such as *The Cowboy and the Señorita*. Later they became sidekicks in real life, tying the knot in 1947. Dale Evans never ranched, never rodeoed. Her ease on horseback came mostly from Hollywood riding lessons, and her western wardrobe was courtesy of the studio costume shop. Dale's hair never seemed to muss when she galloped singing across the prairie with Roy; for that, she credits good hairdressers and lots of hairspray. Sometimes she rode in short skirts, but up on the silver screen Dale never looked worried about her thighs chafing raw in the saddle. Like Roy Rogers, she seemed somehow superhuman, unfazed by wind, blisters, and runaway stagecoaches.

Dale Evans insists she never intended to become "Queen of the West"; it just happened. Born on a ranch in Texas and raised on

THE COWGIRL POET

Doctoring Worms

By Georgie Connell Sicking

You have had some stormy weather
Some good old summer rain.
The grass is draggin' on your stirrups
And cattle on the gain.

The rock holes where the cattle water
Are full and runnin' over
At first glance it looks
Just like everything is clover.

Then you spy a droopy-looking calf
Standing there and then he turns
You might as well get your rope down,
That dogie is full of worms.

You ride up on him sort of easy,
Your horse is walkin' slow.
You build your loop just right
And catch him the first throw.

You would surely hate to chase him
Because he has got 'em pretty bad.
He is weak and kind of little
And lookin' mighty sad.

Then the cook has spanish rice for supper
And it makes your stomach squirm
After ridin' in the summertime
And doctorin' a case of worms.

an Arkansas farm, Dale didn't even arrive in Hollywood until she was nearly thirty years old. Already twice married and the mother of a teenage son, she'd worked as a singer on the radio, and in nightclubs in Chicago, Memphis, and Dallas, before the movies beckoned. Once on the coast, Dale Evans's career simmered on a back burner until Republic Pictures teamed her with Roy Rogers. When the fan mail came pouring in after a couple of westerns, Dale figured that "riding a horse, and occasionally saying 'He went thataway'" wasn't the worst fate that could befall a girl.

Although she racked up thousands of hours of radio time, made scores of movies, and appeared for many years on television, Dale fell somehow short of traffic-stopping celebrity status. Dale Evans comics never sold quite as well as the Roy Rogers series. The Dale Evans watch never buckled around as many little wrists as the Roy model did. Trigger, Roy's four-legged friend, rated co-star billing as "The Smartest Horse in the Movies." Dale's amazing mounts, Pal and later Buttermilk, sometimes didn't get recognized until a film's final credits rolled. Still, for a generation of Americans, those boys and girls who spent the Saturday mornings of their childhoods in the popcorn-scented darkness of the local picture show, Dale Evans—fearless, loyal, outspoken, hard-working, pretty—remains cowgirl incarnate. When we think cowgirl, we conjure images of the Queen of the West.

Some purists insist that the movies injured the cowgirl image, but film actually fermented the cowgirl persona at first, and ultimately altered it just a bit. Perhaps moving pictures even permanently mutated the word "cowgirl" not so much to mean a woman known for the practical work she did, but rather to refer to a certain western-styled female individualist.

The Cowgirl Hall of Fame in Hereford, Texas, recognizes many types of cowgirls—pioneer women, ranchers, rodeo riders, entertainers. Since its founding in 1975 the Hall of Fame has inducted more than one hundred women, both living and dead, as milestone cowgirls—courageous, maverick females who've made a lasting contribution to western heritage. The names of women such as all-around cowgirl Lucille Mulhall, prairie homemaker Molly Goodnight, Wild

Wester Annie Oakley, rodeo star Tad Lucas, writer Willa Cather, and artist Georgia O'Keeffe have been enshrined in the cowgirl Valhalla, where an extensive collection of books, artifacts, and folklore preserve and perpetuate the cowgirl legend.

The Hall of Fame doesn't suggest that the cowgirl is an anachronism or museum relic. Far from it. In Amarillo, about an hour's drive from the Hall of Fame headquarters, a typical day finds cowpoke Cindy Price going to early-morning aerobics, and taking her preschool son to the dentist. Then, while her husband hauls a load of beef-on-the-hoof to market, she lets the horses out of the paddock, repairs a gate blown down by gusty wind, and finishes doctoring an ailing colt just in time to pick up her kids from school. The characters in the movie *Thelma and Louise* portrayed modern-day desperadas, 1990s versions of Belle Starr and Calamity Jane barreling across the West wielding weapons from behind the wheel of a convertible instead of from the backs of fast palominos. More than two thousand women aged ten to seventy-two carry cards certifying membership in the Women's Professional Rodeo Association. One of them, barrel racer Charmayne James Rodman, pockets roughly $100,000 in rodeo prize money each year. Over in Nashville, when singer Reba McEntire takes the stage decked out in her designer western getups, she looks every bit as cowgirl as Annie Oakley or Dale Evans.

Then there are the urban cowgirls. All hat and no cattle, these drugstore cowgirls are secretaries, teachers, lawyers, bankers, and other city-dwelling professionals who favor jeans, boots, and turquoise jewelry as a shortcut subscription to the cowgirl mystique. No less than ranch women and rodeo stars, these city-slicker cowgirls carry the banner once waved by Lucille Mulhall. Cowgirl is as much a spirit as an occupation. Whether riding the range in West Texas, brokering bonds on Wall Street, fishing for marlin in Key West, teaching physics at M.I.T., or walking down a fashion-show runway in Paris, today's cowgirl is where you find her. Proving that you can take the cowgirl out of the Wild West, but you can never, ever take the Wild West out of the cowgirl.

CHAPTER TWO

YOU CAN SEE BY MY OUTFIT

ONE DAY IN 1920, a cowgirl sashayed into Neiman-Marcus and bought $20,000 worth of pretty clothes. The next day she returned and plopped down $20,000 more, spending roughly a quarter of a million of today's dollars in less than forty-eight hours. That cowgirl was Texas ranch heiress Electra Waggoner, a prairie princess famous for her shopping sprees.

Between seasons at Palm Beach and booty-gathering trips to Europe and the Orient, Electra moved into a mansion in Dallas not too far from her beloved Neiman-Marcus. Her palace, called Shadowlawn, stretched three blocks and had a lake in the backyard. Inside, Electra's closet was a warehouse of

chic. One room was filled only with her furs. Another overflowed with more than three hundred and fifty pairs of custom-made shoes. People whispered that new shoes were delivered to Shadowlawn daily, and that designer dresses arrived special freight directly from New York and Paris. Electra Waggoner, you might say, packed a Texas-sized passion for fashion.

Depending on where she lives and how often she's in the saddle, today's cattlewoman might wear anything from a Chanel suit to tight Wranglers and a RODEO NAKED T-shirt. Of course, what hangs in a cattlewoman's closet also has quite a bit to do with whether or not she has any oil under her acreage, and with how many head she runs. Most cattle operations don't build fashion bud-

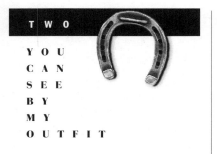

gets as big as Electra Waggoner's unless there's something more lucrative than cows in the rancher's investment portfolio.

But not to worry. The price tags on cowgirl gear feature all numbers of zeros. Affluent ranch women go for brand names and custom-made items. Handcrafted boots from Lucchese are extravagantly expensive, as is a set of luggage ordered special from the King Ranch Saddle Shop. In cattle country, monogrammed leather—saddles, boots, luggage—symbolizes status whether marked with the ranch's brand or the owner's initials. Well-off cowgirls carry their reatas in Louis Vuitton rope cases, and city cowgirl wannabes spend big bucks on designer updates of Old West classics. But many more middle-class buckaroos shop for "loud rags" at K-Mart, at Sears, or at small western-wear stores where the sign says simply: COWBOY BOOTS.

I'd like to buy some boots," a city girl announces to a dapper cowboy behind the counter in a small-town western store. "Some pointy-toe brown boots with a high heel."

"Hmmmm." The retail cowboy seems puzzled. He pushes his hat back on his head. "Pointed toes? You won't find any pointed-toe boots in West Texas, ma'am. We wear round toes and low heels around here. If you want pointed toes you're gonna have to go to Dallas." He chuckles and shakes his head, "Or New York City or somewhere like that. But lemme show you what's hot out here."

They may not be the thing on Fifth Avenue or Rodeo Drive, but the round-toed, low-heeled cowboy boots called "ropers" practically fly off western-wear store shelves these days, especially in areas where real cowboys and cowgirls live and work. The most popular calfskin roper, made by the Justin boot company, comes in twenty or so different colors, ranging from plain brown to neon pink.

A poured-on pair of unusual denim trousers called "chap jeans" perfectly complements a pair of ropers; these snug-fitting ladies' pants have extra flaps of cloth on the front that look something like built-in chaps. And don't bother shopping for basic blue or khaki. Chap jeans and other women's denims come in a rainbow of colors and prints. So do cowboy hats.

Borrowing the same quaint fashion psychology that once dictat-

WOMANLY FOOTWEAR

The cowgirl doesn't own a pair of espadrilles. No strappy sandals. No high-top, air-cushioned, pumped-up, gravity-defying sports shoes either. The cowgirl never darkens the door of Pappagallo or Kenneth Cole. A cowgirl wears boots.

But Imelda Marcos has nothing on the cowgirl clotheshorse. In the footwear department, the prairie princess pulls out something appropriate for all occasions. Shiny black patent-leather boots go to the Cattleman's Ball. Red, white, and blue boots for the Fourth of July. Red and green embossed with holly leaves say it all on Christmas morning. She steps into low-heeled ropers for walking, and tucks her jeans into high-heeled riders for saddle work.

Boots with skirts? Hell, yeah. Dale Evans did it. And Annie Oakley and Lucille Mulhall. Boots with tights? Sure. Boots with shorts? Well, it worked for the Dallas Cowboy cheerleaders, but with chafing in the saddle and brush scratching the legs and all, real cowgirls don't wiggle into hot pants much.

The First Lady of Cowboy Boots, Enid Justin, built an empire of leather and topstitching. Her Nocona Boot Company merged with her brothers' H. J. Justin and Sons in 1981, and before her death in 1990 she was inducted into the National Cowgirl Hall of Fame. When "Miss Enid" drove around Texas in her Cadillac with the license tag EJ BOOT, on the accelerator she rested a feminine foot shod in the most womanly of footwear—an exquisite cowgirl boot.

These Boots Were Made for Riding

26

THE COWGIRL POET

Hey, Cowboy

By Peggy Godfrey

I may not have your anatomy
Nor weigh the pounds you do
But, fella, let me tell ya
I'm not in awe of you.

Winters are cold to both of us
An' both our backs get sore
Old age don't care which sex we are
An' heifers in labor don't score.

The hand that feeds isn't woman or man
It's just the hand that's there
The truck won't start for God, Herself,
You read that right—don't stare.

The hands that rein the gather
Don't have to be a man's
Fencin' tools aren't pink and blue
To specify whose hands.

A green colt isn't more polite
To a woman or a man
Either of the sexes
Can burn a proper brand.

Irrigation waters flood
To bring dry earth to life
Do they ask who's at the headgate
Husband, child, or wife?

My days are long and busy
'Cause I'm livin' from the land
Clothes don't make ya "cowboy"
It's the work that makes a hand.

ed purses and pumps should match, a cutting-edge cowgirl usually chooses a chromatic theme when coordinating an outfit. So purple ropers, with, let's say, peach chap jeans and a purple hat would combine for an eye-catching ensemble. As for shirts and tops, sequins are au courant for barrel racers. And at honky-tonks from Tucson to Texarkana black blouses with sheer chiffon sleeves worn over a visible, lacy black brassiere are all the rage. Whether they are cattlewomen, rodeo queens, movie stars, or city slickers, cowgirls care a lot about clothes. As one shopaholic cowgirl in Dallas says, "Down here we wear our net worth."

The cowgirl's fashion watchwords for the 1990s? Colorful and tight—hues bright enough to taste, pants snug enough to stop circulation. But a century ago, cowpoke couture wasn't nearly so haute.

In the early days, each item in the ranch hand's wardrobe served a specific purpose. The wide-brimmed hat kept the sun off a cowhand's face. The bandanna protected his neck from sunburn, covered his face in a dust storm, kept his running nose dry during cold and flu season, and mopped his tears when a favorite horse headed Up Yonder. High-heeled boots kept a rider's feet securely in the stirrups. Heavy-duty trousers and leather chaps (pronounced *"shaps"* by authentic ranch folks) kept brush from scratching his legs.

Two items from the cowboy's practical wardrobe have become symbols of the American West—the cowboy hat and cowboy boots.

The cowboy hat developed as a hybrid of the slouch hat and the Mexican sombrero. In 1859 John B. Stetson sold his first "big hats" to Colorado gold miners. Just after the Civil War, Stetson's company in Philadelphia began producing a practical hat keeping the special needs of the range rider in mind. In addition to shielding the cowboy's face from the sun with a wide brim, the Stetson's high-crown construction kept his head cool. Satisfied customers called Stetson's innovative head wear "The Boss of the Prairie." The Stetson, available in various brim widths and two colors, black or white, quickly became the cowboy standard. Some hands customized theirs, adding a chin strap to keep it in place on a windy day or tying on a special

AMERICA'S HANDKERCHIEF

The Basic Bandanna: It Isn't Just for Nose-Blowing Anymore

The 22 x 22–inch red cotton square makes a good . . .

- Baby diaper
- Wash cloth
- Coffee filter
- Dog muzzle
- Belt
- Gag
- Hot pad

- Flyswatter
- Coin pouch
- Gas cap
- Small-gift wrap
- Neckerchief
- Cowgirl babushka
- Wide-load indicator

- Distress signal
- Place mat
- Blindfold
- Hobo luggage
- Disguise
- Tourniquet
- Hankie

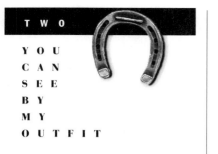

band to help it keep its shape when wet. A good cowboy hat could be expensive, costing the ranch hand perhaps two-thirds of his monthly pay. But the hat supplied much more than portable shade. It could be used to carry water, fan a campfire, signal a colleague, shoo a fly, prod a pokey cow, or cover the eyes during a siesta. To those heading west, a durable Stetson was more than just a hat; it was a ranch implement, a real investment.

The cowboy's boots were not made for walking. They were designed with riding in mind. And since boots served only one real purpose, they were far less costly than the cowboy's versatile hat. In the 1870s a nice pair of boots might set a cowpoke back $7.50, $15 if made to measure. And they didn't look much like the western boots of today. Prototypical cowboy boots closely resembled English-style riding boots. With a rounded toe and forward sloping heel about two inches high, they reached almost to the cowboy's knee. The pointed-toe shape came later when cowboys learned that a point found the stirrup more easily. There were no fancy ostrich- or anaconda- or alligator-hide boots back then, and certainly not anything available in a tangerine shade or a nice chartreuse. Nor could early cowboys be bothered with elaborate tooling or ornamentation. They were too busy taming the frontier to think much about fashion in footwear. Just plain leather boots, brown or black.

Cowboy boots carried many different brand names. But in the same way "Stetson" became a generic term for a cowboy hat, "Levi's" became a popular synonym for cowboy pants. Levi Strauss stitched up his first pair of tough trousers for miners during the California gold rush of 1849. The rugged sailcloth used in Strauss's britches was called "cloth *de Nîmes*" after the city in France where it was made. Denim, *de Nîmes*, get it? Miners wore Levi's because the copper rivets kept the pockets from tearing when they bulged with ore samples. Cowboys wore Levi's because they were long-lasting. Women wore Levi's at their own risk.

A western historian once wrote that any woman heading west dressed in silks and satins was immediately suspected of being a prostitute. A respectable pioneer woman was expected to wear work clothes, at least until she completed the journey westward. Even once

Welcome to my humble chapeau

It's more than a hat. It's a ranching implement

Bad Gals Wear Black.
Resistol 20x Black Gold

Good Gals Wear White.
Stetson 20x White Cloud

Cattlewoman's Classic.
Resistol 30x Beaver

Horsewoman's Special.
Resistol 5x

they'd set up homesteads, rural western women favored functional clothing. But in the latter half of the 1800s, work clothes didn't translate into jeans and a T-shirt. For Prairie Madonnas and early female cowboys, long skirts, long-sleeved blouses, shawls, and sunbonnets were the order of the day.

Since most of a pioneer cowgirl's chores were done far from the judgmental eyes of town folk, she soon began appropriating some of the more practical items from the cowboy's closet, in the interest of comfort and convenience. The first female cowhands sported wide-brimmed cowboy hats, riding boots, bandannas. And very, very occasionally—if she was truly a rebel—a cowgirl would wear trousers. Even in a rough-and-tumble fledgling society like that of the developing American West, a woman in britches raised eyebrows. There were a few tough old gals who cared more about comfort than convention. But

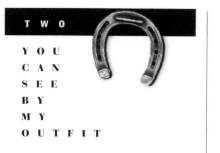

colorful, in-your-face characters like Calamity Jane and Sally Scull, who reputedly favored pants instead of skirts, were a minority. Most women compromised, choosing long skirts stitched up the middle like culottes as work wear, since riding astride was pretty much impossible when encumbered by an ankle-length swatch of wool. Cowgirling, it's easy to imagine, could be difficult when sitting a horse sidesaddle.

Pants on women were a no-no well into this century. Watch a 1930s movie: Katharine Hepburn drew comment when she wore slacks, no matter how sexy. It was deemed a sacrifice of femininity for the good of the country when Rosie the Riveter and other patriotic gals helping with the war effort of the 1940s were permitted to wear coveralls while working on the assembly line. Trousers as acceptable public attire represent a relatively recent stride for women. Remember the pantsuit revolution? Even in the early 1970s girls wearing slacks were sent home from public schools to change into something more appropriate. And women wearing trousers to the office—well, it was scandalous well into the Nixon years.

As iconoclastic as some early cowgirls were—already drawing the wrath of proper Victorians by doing "men's" work—many feared that wearing "men's" clothes would simply add grist to the rumor mill. Cattlewoman Alice Stillwell Henderson devised a way to please everybody. She wore pants down on the ranch, but when she went into town she pulled a long skirt on over them. When Wild West shows and rodeos began taking cowgirls off the range and thrusting them into the limelight, work clothes became costumes. At first the no-pants taboo was honored by Wild Westers, though generally speaking long skirts and rodeo riding didn't mix.

Then Jazz Age flappers popularized bloomers and bared knees, and this meant good news for cowgirls. Bloomers of corduroy or satin, blouses with low necklines, and long ringlet curls peeking out from beneath wide-brimmed western hats was *the* cowgirl look of the 1920s. Fed up with skirts, trick rider Vera McGinnis did bloomers one better. Taking a pair of men's white trousers, she removed the front fly, improvised a new fastener on the side, and created quite a stir wearing her modified menswear at the Fort Worth Rodeo of 1927.

Jodhpurs caught on with cowgirls during the 1930s, changing the approach to equestrienne fashion altogether. Split skirts and bloomers represented attempts to make women's clothes more masculine and better suited for riding, but with the advent of jodhpurs, cowgirls began feminizing men's clothing instead.

After World War II, women's western wear entered the modern era with yokes in pants and shirts, fitted rather than blousing sleeves, elaborate decoration, and denim as the favored fabric of the horsey set. Even though trends in cowgirl wardrobes seemed pretty universal, cowgirl individualists often added their own special flourishes. Bernice Taylor, aka "The Gardenia Lady," always wore a white flower in her hair during her rodeo rides. Another arbiter of taste, Kitty Canutt, sported a small diamond set into a front tooth for a look that was both dubiously decorative and practical. Whenever Kitty's career took a downturn, she'd simply have the diamond removed and pawn it to cover rodeo entry fees. Later, when she was winning, she'd have the stone reset. Pioneer bronc rider Ruth Roach wore her heart on her boots; her trademark was a valentine shape embossed in the leather.

As pretty and stylish as some cowgirls were, as a group they gained a reputation as masculine, hard-looking women. But as one cowboy said of a female colleague: "If she looks tough or mean, it's because her lips are too chapped to smile." The word "rough" didn't

TIGHTEN UP

Snug, but snug enough?

A cowgirl knows her Wranglers fit just right, if . . .

- She has to lie down to zip them.
- It is impossible to slip a business card into her back pocket.
- She plans ahead to sit down.
- She dreads going to the ladies' room.
- Her legs go to sleep when she sits too long.
- "Wedgies" would be redundant.
- She cannot tuck in a blouse.
- Seams are still imprinted on her skin the next morning.
- She can't get money from her pocket without first removing her pants.
- She worries whether tight jeans cause sterility in women.

FRIED, DYED, & SHOVED TO THE SIDE

The Cowgirl's Big Hair

THE BOUFFANT, the Beehive, the Flip, the Bubble—even the hair is big out West. In cattle country big hair is everywhere, but western women aren't the only Americans still wearing their wigs weighty. In the Northeast the large locks tower up. In the Deep South hairdos spread horizontal. Even among cowgirls, a variety of styles huddle beneath the big-hair umbrella.

• **Hair as a Force of Nature:** As one cowgirl's barber observed: "I've teased hair so high it looked like Vesuvius erupting." The real monuments —four feet high, three feet wide, shellacked, and baked to glossy pinnacles—aren't that common anymore. But those not-so-subtle "Priscilla Presley Specials" or "Tiajuana Fantasies," as one stylist calls them, remain the foundation of all big-hair technology.

• **Prayer Hair:** Hairdos from Heaven, never cut or even trimmed. Citing the Bible, specifically I Corinthians, as the divine source of their grooming inspiration, certain apostolic congregations believe a woman's hair is "given for her glory by God" and should never be cut. Therefore, a lifetime of hair is wound around or piled up on the sisters' holy heads—split ends and all. Wearers include female members of United Pentecostal Churches and followers of other apostolic movements. This inconvenient scripture is bad news for some pious cowgirls, because Prayer Hair won't fit under the Stetson.

• **Honky-Tonk Haystacks:** This down-home breed of bouffant is a little rougher looking than geometric big hair, possibly because the honky-tonk angel's halo gets windblown when she rides in the back of the pickup truck. Farrah Fawcett made it popular, and rodeo star Charmayne James proves it's no flash-in-the-pan. Wearers include cowgirls, good ol' gals and Reba clones at kicker clubs across America.

- **Beauty Pageant Insurance:** You won't see a Dorothy Hamill cut in Atlantic City. Miss America, Mrs. America, Miss Rodeo America—at pageants across the land, big hair triumphs every time. "I like my hair teased," said one aging beauty queen, "teased and sort of matted, like Trigger's tail."

•

One stylist out West says the trick to pleasing his cowgirl clientele lies in the back-combing technique. Sometimes, he even puts his rattail comb aside and teases with his fingers: the beauty operator's equivalent of skiing barefoot.

There's big, then there's BIG. When a gal in Houston requested "big ol' hair" from her beautician, he complied like a New York cabbie instructed to hurry: "Honey, I teased that hair all the way to Dallas." And if asked, he could have taken it clear on to Tulsa.

usually come up in descriptions of Lucille Mulhall; perhaps to offset her tomboy vocation, Lucille favored a feminine coiffure. She pulled her long blond curls back away from her face with a ribbon. Beginning with Lucille and continuing even today with current rodeo champ Charmayne Rodman and others, there remains one colossal fashion "don't" among cowgirls: *Don't* get your hair cut short. Cowgirls oppose the Dorothy Hamill look. Or the Princess Diana cut. Or the Sinead O'Connor. They prefer their hair long, and probably always will. Why? It looks better under the hat.

There's a correlative cowgirl hair "do" as well: *Do* perm, tease, and mousse it to the moon. On Long Island and in New Jersey the big hair goes vertical. In the cities of the South big hair bulges horizontally. But on ranches and in rodeo arenas throughout the southwest, big hair spills down and spreads wide like an unkempt haystack. A Louisiana cowboy, allergic to mousse and gel hair preparations, says he must be careful when choosing dancing partners in country-and-western nightclubs. The more attractive the cowgirl, the more he sneezes.

Three things turn a cowgirl's head: a cowboy, a good-looking horse, and a sale at Sheplers. A cornucopia of boots and hats and saddles, the flagship store in Wichita, Kansas, is to western wear what Bergdorf Goodman is to haute couture. Inhaling a whiff of the place is like experiencing the very best of barnyard aromas. A heady scent of wood and leather—this is the way a ranch might smell if it was air-conditioned and dung-free.

This fifty-thousand-square-foot retail Ponderosa is the showpiece of the chain, the largest western-wear outlet in the nation. The majority of Sheplers' nineteen stores are near metropolitan areas, but since ranching is a rural industry, the company mails out eighteen million catalogs each year as well. Ranchers refer to the Sheplers catalog as the "cowboy's wish book." And the stores? Well, with shelves of boots, acres of Wranglers, loads of Levi's, Stetsons, bolo ties, fancy belts, spurs—Sheplers makes a fashion-conscious cowpoke who ambles in think she's gone on to her final reward.

Consider this sartorial math: Wrangler, the purveyor of official pro rodeo denims, sells about 60 million pairs of jeans annually. The Tony Lama Boot Company ships around 700,000 pairs of boots per year. An industry spokesman estimates recent Sheplers' sales in the vicinity of $130 million per year. Not included in those numbers are myriad other western items. Short pleated skirts printed with Wild West scenes were popular a few seasons ago. The J. Peterman Company, a mail-order clothier, was built around the $184 cowboy duster. A western-themed charm bracelet can set a cowgirl back $85 to $140 at a western collectibles shop in Houston.

Some ranch women don't get to town too often. But when they do, they're apt to study city fashion trends with voracious gusto. Coupling the latest styles from New York and Paris with their own cowgirl staples, cattlewomen sometimes spawn unique new looks, such as a flouncy miniskirt with a straw cowboy hat or battered boots.

The less affluent cowgirl might get to the mall even less frequently than the cattle baroness. If her herd is small and her property oil-free, the middle-class cowgirl probably makes her clothing decisions based more upon what rides well than what looks good. Among her crowd a pair of denims, basic boots, and a cotton shirt never go out of style. But then again, her crowd mostly eats grass and goes moo.

If the cattlewoman leans toward pricy, understated quality in clothing, and the not-so-wealthy cowgirl opts for functional, affordable durability, the rodeo cowgirl reaches for glitter and flash when getting dressed. Like a Las Vegas dancer, the barrel racer wants to show pretty under the lights. Although she is constantly on the road, the rodeo cowgirl's world seems small simply because she interacts mostly with other rodeo cowgirls. Therefore, the barrel racer's wardrobe represents cowgirl chic at its purest because it's seldom influenced by other styles.

To understand rodeo fashion you must understand tight jeans, the building block of all the barrel racer's outfits. Believe it or not, snug britches bring better rides. Competitors insist that if pants are baggy they tend to creep up on the cowgirl's legs when she's in the

BIG BALLS IN COWTOWN

Gettin' Gussied Up for the Cattle Baron's Bash

In Dallas it's an institution. Twice it's been held at South Fork—the ranch house used for exterior shots of J. R. Ewing's television manor. And sometimes Larry Hagman attends along with Linda Gray and Patrick Duffy and other famous fictional Dallasites.

The ball benefits cancer research. Tickets start at $350 per person for the back-forty tables, and prime seating costs $1,200 per cowboy.

At the first Cattle Baron's Ball more than twenty years ago, most of the revelers opening their billfolds to battle disease were rich ranchers. These days the ranch folk still attend, but many more urban cowgirls and drugstore cowboys grace the guest list. Foreign media loves the outdoor spectacle, especially the Germans, who always send at least one television news crew to cover the event.

Cattle Baron's is officially a casual affair—but a curious brand of casual. Last year, one cowgirl-for-a-day wore the white suede wedding dress used in *Dances with Wolves*. "She borrowed the dress," one socialite says, "and I heard that she had to sign a waiver with the insurance people promising that she wouldn't drink red wine while wearing it." The ball is not a costume affair, but one woman climbed out of her limo at Cattle Baron's last summer dressed as an Old West saloon keeper. Another came as an Indian princess. Suede is a popular fabric at the ball—suede halters, suede skirts, leather pants—even though the temperature at party time usually hovers near 100 degrees. Last year one cowgirl ate brisket in the blazing Texas sun with a feather boa wrapped around her neck. Why? "It just looked sooo darling with my new boots, " the cowgirl said. As she proudly displayed a pair of rhinestone-encrusted boots, a bead of sweat rolled slowly down her nose and into her potato salad.

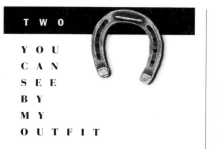

saddle. Snug jeans aren't specifically required for rodeo entry, but the Women's Professional Rodeo Association does prescribe a dress code for members to follow in competition. Plain blue denim jeans are not permitted; colors only. Blouses must be long-sleeved and buttoned up the front. Infractions of the dress-code draw fines from the central office; so do other little cowgirl faux pas, such as losing a hat in the arena during a run.

Barrel racers frequently buy plain shirts and then have them customized with sequins and glitter and colorful appliqués. A woman in Waco built a cottage industry by simply sewing sparkles onto off-the-rack blouses for rodeo gals. Elaborate earrings nicely dress up a rodeo ensemble. And nothing screams "cowgirl" quite like a salad-plate-sized belt buckle. The sterling silver National Finals Rodeo buckle has become the sorority pin of the barrel circuit. Any competitor worth her horse's hay proudly wears that big slab of silver right over her navel wherever she goes.

So knock ranch wear up a notch or two on the flash meter and it becomes rodeo wear; slide the rodeo look down just a decibel or so and you have show-business cowgirl couture. Cowgirl entertainers usually eschew tight jeans and big buckles in favor of more feminine skirts and dresses. To keep a Hollywood cowgirl quiet on the set, just hang a fringed skirt and vest, and maybe a hat with a chin strap, in her dressing room.

That same fashion song plays backstage in Nashville too. Dolly Parton usually takes the stage wearing some variation of the prairie skirt. Patsy Cline, the premier cowgirl chanteuse of the 1950s, originated a style perhaps best described by the oxymoron "sophisticated country," sort of a Dale Evans meets Jackie Kennedy kind of thing. When Patsy appeared at the Grand Ole Opry she modeled sleek, tailored sequined gowns, a bouffant hairdo, and nosebleed-high spike-heeled shoes. Her look hinted at the cosmopolitan, but her sound was tinged with country.

Look around at the Million Dollar Cowboy Bar in Jackson Hole, Wyoming. Check out the wait staff at the chili bar in the Red Sage restaurant in Washington, D.C. Spend an afternoon at the bull-riding contest down in Del Rio, Texas—and you'll see that cowgirls are clotheshorses. Sometimes cowgirls look so swell in their fringe and boots that other women—gals who wouldn't look twice at a roan quarter horse and would turn and run from a calving cow—adopt cowgirl regalia, too. Cowboy boots are like chicken pox: everybody has 'em at least once.

For many people that first taste of western chic creates a hunger for the hard stuff. A pair of snazzy boots cry out for a flashy belt. And that belt would really dress up a pair of turquoise jeans. Then, for rainy days, there's the must-have long cowboy duster. Next thing you know, you're wondering if that duster could be ordered in turquoise to match the jeans.

In San Antonio the pony-tailed Junior League mom type will

often add just a touch of cowgirlishness to her casual wear. Climbing out of her Suburban, she might sport a long sarong skirt in a campy 1950s-style cowboy print, a denim work shirt with the sleeves rolled up, silver bracelets and earrings, huarache sandals, and the ubiquitous King Ranch Saddle Shop *la bolsa*—a monogrammed purse made from the material used in convertible car tops and trimmed in leather. Cowhide belts decorated with sterling-silver conchos are also seen far from the ranch, as are fancy boots peeking out from beneath longish chambray prairie skirts.

So stylish are American cowgirls they are imitated around the world. Most major national women's magazines have run spreads on cowgirl-inspired couture featuring women in designer outfits and cowboy hats. In Italy, trick roper Nancy Kelley Sheppard provided cowgirl entertainment during a Giorgio Armani fashion show, and in Paris, Czechoslovakian-born divorcée Ivana Trump strutted down the planks at Thierry Mugler's ready-to-wear show in a cowgirlish silver-sequined gown.

On Main Street in Santa Monica, miles from the nearest cattle-grazing ground or rodeo arena, a shop called Bootz sells designer cowboy gear. In Manhattan at Billy Martin's on Madison Avenue, members of the button-down pinstriped set buy spurs. Ralph Lauren, a handsome Jewish fellow from the Bronx, has become America's most authentic-

Trick roper Nancy Kelley Sheppard.

looking cowboy. Besides Lauren, other designer's recent collections have drawn on whimsical cowgirl themes, with bandanna-print sarongs for the pavement prairie. It's not just a trend among grownups either. On one television talk show, a woman who studies the psychological effects of clothing on children said the cowgirl look is big with the urban junior high set. At Jackson Hole, a popular New York hamburger hangout, a teenager from a nearby private school sips a soda with her pals. She wears vintage cowboy boots with her tartan school-uniform skirt.

You don't have to be a sociologist to decipher the continuing popularity of cowgirl and cowboy clothing. It's not the boots and hats themselves that are so appealing, it's what they symbolize. Western wear stands for cowboys and cowgirls, and cowboys and cowgirls are equated with courage, bravery, integrity, and pioneer spirit.

Another trend in western wear glorifies the concept of hand-me-downs. Vintage cowboy boots, 1950s yoked shirts, and preworn fringed jackets have become sought-after items. In Austin, a place called Cadillac Jack's sells used boots and chaps and hats to college students, business people, and movie costume departments. Some of the footwear for sale at Cadillac Jack's once covered famous feet—the store's vault contains a pair of Elvis's cowboy boots. Most pairs, however, served anonymous cowpokes through years of ranch work. As far as broken-in comfort and character go, new boots can't touch preworns.

Also in Austin, cotton wrap-around skirts printed with western scenes are way cool on the campus of the University of Texas. A Wall Street analyst packs her exercise wear into a cloth overnight bag decorated with illustrations of cowboys on horseback. In a restaurant in Los Angeles, a middle-aged real-estate lady produces contracts from a leather portfolio decorated with saddle tooling. Even television's Murphy Brown has some cowgirl in her closet; in one episode she wore a maternity blouse decorated with a western motif. Perhaps there's a cowgirl corner in so many women's closets because there's a bit of cowgirl in so many women.

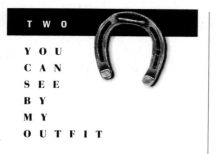

As big as the living room of a double-wide mobile home, the closet where Fern Sawyer hangs her duds could qualify as a museum of cowgirl clothing. Fern's one hundred pairs of boots are stored in a revolving barrel-shaped chest. More than half of them were custom-made. She calls one pair, decorated with hearts and spades and clubs and diamonds, "my Vegas boots." Do they bring her luck at the blackjack table? "Not particularly, but they bring compliments from the other gamblers."

For Fern, cowboy boots are womanly footwear. Another pair is red, white, and blue, Old Glory for the feet; she wears them on the Fourth of July. Fern owns a pair of pink boots, a pair of bright green, and a pair that glow in the dark. Then there are the hats—twenty-five or so of them. "You know, your hat has got to match your boots." And the evening wear—a full rack of sequins, a couple of Oscar de la Rentas and some Halstons. "He died, you know," Fern says of Halston. "My real favorite is Galanos. Ooooh, I love his stuff."

In the foyer of the Sawyer hacienda hangs a framed page from a 1940 edition of the Fort Worth *Star-Telegram* with an enormous photo of impeccably-dressed Fern, aged twenty-five. The headline says: COWGIRLS RISE IN POPULARITY. "Yeah," she jokes, "I guess I was dressing like a cowgirl the first time it was cool."

Today Fern maintains three separate wardrobes. "One for work, one for western dress-up, one for regular ladylike stuff," she explains. While pointing out the nuances of her collection, Fern sports faded jeans, a work shirt, and scuffed cowboy boots—plain brown, round-toed, low-heeled boots. "I don't do pointed toes," she says, "unless I'm dressing up, stepping out in New York or Dallas."

When in Dallas, Fern has been known to drop big bucks at Neiman-Marcus from time to time as well. Like prairie princess Electra Waggoner, Fern Sawyer is a cowgirl with a penchant for fashion.

CHAPTER THREE

LITTLE HOUSES ON THE PRAIRIE

A MERE HOUSE can seldom hold a cowgirl's heart in the way, say, a herd of choice Charolais can. If images of the green, green grass of home happen to make an otherwise stoic cowgirl turn sentimental and misty, it's because to her way of thinking the green, green grass *is* home.

Now this is not to imply that the average female cowpoke sleeps in lush pastureland or receives mail addressed "Back Forty, Under the Mesquite." But just because she bunks under a roof doesn't mean that the cowgirl holds the place in the same regard most other women might. To a cowgirl, home makes a handy place for hanging a hat and resting

one's bones between the end of evening chores and the start of morning rounds. One young cowgirl put it best when she said, "This house doesn't pay for the ranch."

This probably comes as no news flash. The woman who warms to worming calves and dehorning steers doesn't often bring the same enthusiasm to interior decorating and swapping recipes at the Piggly Wiggly. Quite often the gal with a meticulously organized barn, smooth-running pickup truck, and paddock of perfectly groomed quarter horses is the very same woman who has a carton of blinky milk in her refrigerator, dirty laundry overflowing the hamper, and scuff marks on her coffee table. It boils down

to a question of priorities. To the cowgirl, housekeeping doesn't rate a spot near the top of the list.

Walk into a cowgirl's house, any cowgirl's house, and ten-to-one the first thing she'll say is "excuse the mess." Housekeeping apologies, like big belt buckles and suntans, seem pretty much ubiquitous on the prairie. "Oh, just move that rope and those spurs off the sofa; we weren't expecting company." Sometimes a cluttered ranch house

BREAKFAST OF CHAMPIONS

Chewy Coffee and Bite-Back Biscuits

Forget about Wheaties. No croissant or fresh-squeezed OJ. Western omelet? Not hardly. Classic continental breakfast in a cattle camp consists of coffee, biscuits, and sometimes a cigarette.

Texas rancher Hallie Stillwell learned the hard way about just how particular cowpokes can be about that first cup o'joe at sunup. When newlywed, Hallie set out to clean the kitchen where her new husband and his hired hands had been rustling up their grub. She encountered a filthy black coffeepot that looked as if it had never seen soapy water. Trying to be helpful, Hallie pulled out the steel wool and scrubbed the pot till it gleamed. Her husband and the ranch hands fumed when they saw what she'd done. "Hell," one aggravated cowboy said, "it'll be six months before this pot can make decent coffee again."

Hallie Stillwell's Dirty-Pot, Crack-of-Dawn, High-Octane Coffee

14 cups cold water
2 eggs
2 cups ground coffee
Large kettle
Medium-sized mixing bowl
14-cup coffeepot.

Pour 12 cups of water into the kettle and bring to a boil. In the bowl, mix a mush of the eggs and crushed eggshells, one cup of water, and two cups of ground coffee. Dump the mushy mixture into the coffeepot. Plug the pot's spout with paper to trap aroma and flavor, then pour the boiling water over the mush. Stir, cover, and boil for three minutes. Before serving, pour one cup of cold water into pot to settle grounds.

Vera McGinnis had no trouble brewing up stout ranchland java; biscuits were her downfall. One winter when Vera and her husband were homesteading in Wyoming, an unexpected visitor stopped in to say howdy. Vera attempted to whip up a fast batch of biscuits. Feeling pleased with herself, she presented a plate of rather flat but golden bread patties to her guest. The fellow's face turned sour after his first bite. Vera had used baking *soda* instead of baking *powder*, leaving her cowboy snacks mighty bitter tasting, and sort of yellow and raw inside.

Vera McGinnis' Real Fast, Real Good, No-Soda Biscuits*

2 cups all-purpose flour
1 tablespoon baking powder
2 teaspoons sugar
1 teaspoon salt
1/4 cup shortening
3/4 cup milk

Mix dry ingredients. Work in shortening. Add liquid. Knead into soft dough. Pinch dough into balls, place in well-greased pan. Cook at 400° till brown.

* An Easier Way: Make dough by mixing Bisquick and water in a plastic bag. Then wad dough around a stick and hold over campfire until golden brown. Serve with syrup.

cries out for some sort of explanation. "I've been busy with calving and haven't had a minute to get to those dishes." Other times the homestead practically sparkles, but the cowgirl still comments on the clutter, as if her lack of domestic skill stands out as some sort of congenital defect. The omnipresent "excuse the mess," translates as the cowgirl's way of saying, "I know other people put a premium on things like a ring-free bathtub, but I don't. Hope it doesn't offend."

Modern range homesteads come in two basic varieties: the Ranch Trailer and the Big Hacienda. Generally speaking, there's nothing in between. It doesn't take a MENSA member to figure which belongs to the cowgirl and which to the cattlewoman. For the trailer-dwelling cowgirl, comfort and convenience come first; appearance matters little or not at all. The ranch wife or cattlewoman tends to stack her priorities the other way around.

The earliest American ranch dwellings went up as little more than barns for humans. Pioneer ranchers, seeking protection from the weather as well as from wild animals and outlaws, considered any shelter good shelter. Comfort was at best a secondary concern, and aesthetics didn't enter the mix at all. The materials used varied from region to region. Dugouts or standard sod houses could be erected almost anywhere. Rocks made sturdy homes in Texas. Adobe worked well in New Mexico and other parts of the desert Southwest. Traditional log cabins sprang up near evergreen forests.

Most early ranch houses shared a similar floor plan. In many, two to four rooms surrounded an interior courtyard, where domestic tasks could be performed safely. Others typically consisted of a single room with thick walls, dirt floor, and sometimes a few small windows. Bedrooms were uncommon even in frontier-town residences until the mid-1800s. On the prairie a proper bed made a home really deluxe, even ostentatious. A crude shack sometimes also served as a makeshift office where an early rancher might scrawl breeding records and other important herd information directly onto the walls or rafters of his home. (As a bride in 1918, Hallie Stillwell got the silent treatment from her husband after she scrubbed the graffiti from the walls. New to the ranch, Hallie didn't realize that the scrib-

FROM THE LA-Z-BOY I SEE...

Ah! the Great Indoors

- A super-deluxe, twenty-five-inch, stereo, color TV
- Two-tone shag carpeting
- Wood-look wall paneling
- Rodeo trophies
- Bag of Chee-tos
- Can of bean dip
- Sofa upholstered in the "hide of the stately Naugha"
- Copy of "The Cowboy's Prayer" mounted on a chunk of wood
- Charles M. Russell poster in plastic frame
- Doggie chew-toy
- Back issue of *The Cattleman* magazine
- Dead house plant
- Pair of mud-caked cowboy boots
- Fancy mirror with an old-time Jack Daniel's ad etched on it
- Empty beer cans on the coffee table
- Play pen (with baby)
- Bridle draped from a coat rack
- Horseshoe above the door
- A needlepoint wall hanging: GOD BLESS THIS MESS

bling represented the cattle company's files.) Most cowboys and ranchers, accustomed to neither roof nor walls, found indoor living—no matter how rudimentary—to be positively swank.

While the earliest cowboys usually wandered as rootless bachelors, bedding down in raucous bunkhouses, second- and third-generation cattle raisers occasionally had a family's safety and comfort to consider. And so the barns for humans slowly developed into cozy little houses on the prairie.

In an effort toward more gracious living, rows of poplars were planted nearby to create cool evening shade. Store-bought or homemade beds and chairs took the place of bedrolls and log stools. Plumbing brought running water into ranch kitchens and made outhouses obsolete. Gas appliances moved most cooking and food preparation indoors as well. Electricity and telephone service arrived late to remote ranching areas, but by the 1950s many rural residences felt every bit as comfortable and modern as big-city homes.

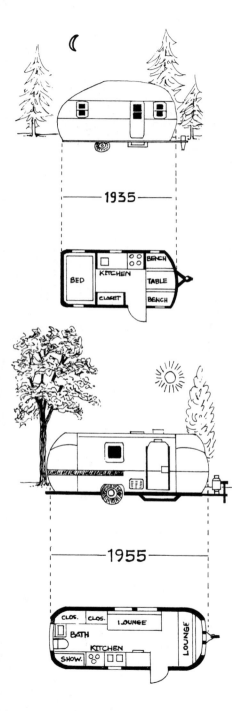

1935

1935

BED KITCHEN BENCH
TABLE
CLOSET BENCH

1955

CLOS. CLOS. LOUNGE
BATH LOUNGE
KITCHEN
SHOW.

The long, low-slung design of ranch headquarters so inspired architects and residential planners that a ranch-style craze took hold in suburbs across America. By the 1950s "ranchettes" fit ten to a city block; cookie-cutter imitations of the functional houses built on the range popped up on half-acre "spreads" on the fringes of almost every American city.

Meanwhile back at the ranch—the real one with cows—another housing trend was taking hold. The mobile home was going up on blocks.

The cattlewoman might hang her hat at the Big Hacienda, but the cowgirl's dream home is double wide and mobile: a 2,100-square foot Redman Shadowridge right off the assembly line, complete with extra insulation, Jacuzzi, and prefab fireplace. Interpret "dream" as fantasy in this case, because that particular top-of-the-line Shadowridge can carry a price tag in the $60,000 vicinity. That's why the average cowgirl and her mister might settle on the more reasonable Kirkwood model, two bedrooms, two baths, with all the options. They could buy it from a smooth-talking dealer named Big Bob at a sales lot on the interstate for $2,500 down plus easy monthly payments of $320 for the next fifteen years. Big Bob just might throw in the delivery and setup for free. The new home-owners could then park and anchor their love nest near the pecan grove just yards from the decaying stone house where their fore-bears once lived. Most of their ranch neighbors probably subscribe to prefabricated living, too. Apparently double-wide aluminum is the design nine out of ten ranchers recommend most.

At the same time that ranch style spread like a house afire in the suburbs, mobile homesteading was altering the look of the range. The mobile home arrived as the bastard child of the house and the automobile. At first, using aircraft technology, the Airstream Corporation pioneered the travel trailers of the 1930s. More transportation than dwelling, the early streamlined trailers were created primarily for mobility. But by the 1950s some travel trailer designers let the home idea supersede the mobility angle. And so the industry split: travel trailers for recreation on the one side, and housing assembled off site on the other.

THE GOOD LIFE CIRCA 1955

Meanwhile, Back at the Ranchette

Bonanza *and TV Dinners in a Ranch-Style Dream Home*

Instead of forty acres and a mule, post–World War II pioneers staking claims in the suburbs hankered for a half acre and a Chevy. On those residential "spreads," 1950s families erected ultra-modern ranch-style homes.

One story. Brick, or maybe aluminum siding. Low-pitched cedar-shake roof with exaggerated eaves. Parallel to the street. Garage at one end. A long, narrow hallway leading to the bedrooms and baths at the other. Two bay windows, a broad picture window, and plain entryway on the façade. Sliding glass door leading to the back patio. Knotty-pine paneled den, probably furnished with his and her La-Z-Boy recliners facing a Curtis Mathes TV with rabbit ears on top.

Ring a bell? Welcome to horizontal heaven. Suburban living with a western flare. One million of these houses went up each year from 1948 to 1950, most of them miles and miles from the nearest cow.

You probably grew up in a "ranch." Or your grandparents lived in one. Today, real-estate agents sometimes throw around words like "rambling" and "California Vernacular" and "Contractor Modern" when reeling in a ranch-style sale. And the ranch-style home now comes in a variety of flavors. There's the standard ranch; the minimal ranch (without an attached garage); the composite ranch (instead of the regular I-shape, it's T-shaped or L-shaped); the split-level ranch; the raised ranch; and the ranch bungalow—which is more or less a standard ranch simply turned the other way to fit a smaller lot.

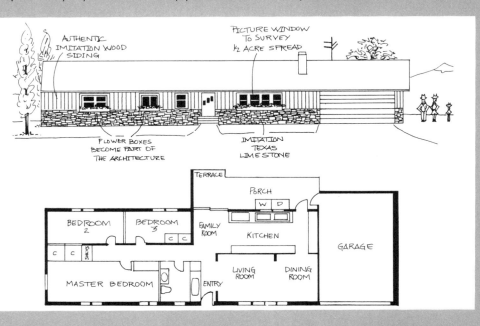

AUTHENTIC IMITATION WOOD SIDING

PICTURE WINDOW TO SURVEY ½ ACRE SPREAD

FLOWER BOXES BECOME PART OF THE ARCHITECTURE

IMITATION TEXAS LIMESTONE

TERRACE

PORCH

W   D

BEDROOM 2

BEDROOM 3

C   C

FAMILY ROOM

KITCHEN

GARAGE

C   C   SHELVES

LIVING ROOM

DINING ROOM

MASTER BEDROOM

ENTRY

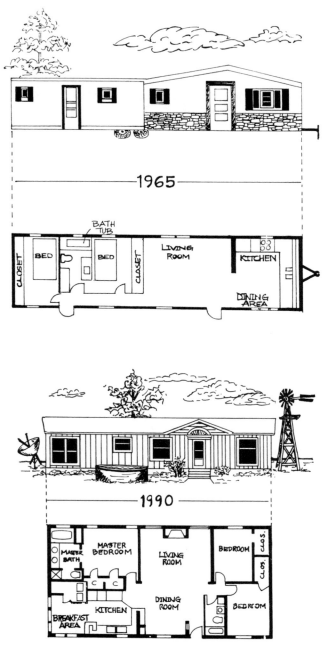

1965

BATH
TUB

CLOSET

BED

BED

CLOSET

LIVING
ROOM

KITCHEN

DINING
AREA

1990

MASTER
BATH

MASTER
BEDROOM

LIVING
ROOM

BEDROOM

CLOS.

CLOS.

DINING
ROOM

BEDROOM

KITCHEN

BREAKFAST
AREA

"Mobile home" might sound like an oxymoron to city dwellers and suburbanites, since "home" represents something attached to the land, and "mobile" suggests practically the opposite. But the word combination poses no problem to farmers and ranchers and other country folk. They consider the land itself to be their permanent home, and a house to be simply temporary shelter.

Texas cowgirl Rebecca Gonzales bunks in a manufactured domicile. On a mountaintop in Arizona, trick roper Nancy Kelley Sheppard lives in customized double-wide comfort too. Even though their nests match thousands of others coming off the assembly line, these cowgirls have taken great pains to personalize their living spaces by adding some nifty flourishes inside and out.

Typically the cowgirl, or her husband, will dress up the front of a mobile home with a screened porch or a basic open-air stoop. Then they'll tack an aluminum carport onto one end of the trailer so they can leave saddles and other valuables in the pickup truck even when it rains. Behind the Ranch Trailer a ten-foot satellite dish supplies the family an electronic window on the world by way of 150 television channels. On the horizon a thousand-gallon cattle-watering tank works just fine as the family swimming pool, made even cooler with the addition of a sun deck installed by Sears. Most mobile homes leave the factory with an interior package such as "Mediterranean" or "Early American," which includes certain color schemes, wall coverings, counter tops, and optional furniture combos.

The Gonzales's carpet is blue, their living-room sofa an earth-tone plaid. A baby swing now rocks back and forth beside mom's deep purple easy chair. Rebecca and her husband Richard added a daughter,

THROW ANOTHER HOG ON THE FIRE

The Prairie Social Scene

When ranch gals heave a slab of meat onto the grill and put the coffee on, home entertainment sometimes enters new frontiers. Chances are the cowgirl prefers being a guest to being a hostess. But every now and again she has to mix up some onion dip and call her kinfolk. Before a party at the Ranch Trailer, the cowgirl makes the bed, picks up the dirty towels off the bathroom floor, buys some chips, ices down a couple of cases of beer, puts a George Strait CD on the stereo, freshens her makeup—and it's showtime.

At a Ranch Trailer hootenany in Oklahoma not long ago, party guests got restless and slaughtered a hog. They butchered it, dug a hole, built a fire, and proceeded to slow-cook the animal the hard way. Since it takes roughly fourteen hours to prepare a pork roast like this, the hostess had to go buy more beer and open a few more bags of chips.

Things aren't nearly so laid back at the Big Hacienda, or "Swankienda" as some say, where social gatherings come in two sizes—big and obscenely big. The cattlewoman's prep work includes calling the caterer, calling the bus company or aircraft charter scheduled to bring guests in from San Antonio or Tulsa or Phoenix, calling George Strait's people to be sure he'll begin performing on time, shopping for a new outfit, and having her hairdresser come early to work his magic with the teasing comb before other guests arrive.

At a July Fourth picnic on a big spread down in Texas, a certain cattlewoman invited a thousand or so of her closest pals out for a little barbecue. Since it was a patriotic holiday, this hostess directed that a portion of her herd of white Charolais cattle be dyed red and blue. Hired helicopters then flew guests over the pasture to see the bovine flag waving across the prairie below.

their first child, to the family not long ago. With only one tiny additional tenant, the mobile home bulges at the seams, literally. "You know, these things are flimsy. Not made very well," Rebecca explains. She and Richard have already been shopping for something new. "Next time we want a double-wide. I saw one I like. It had really great fake mosaic tile in the kitchen—plastic stuff, but sure pretty."

Nancy Sheppard's place is actually two homes shoved together, a customized setup built to her specifications. The factory installed the imitation-plank wall paneling, carpet in the living room, and kitchen Formica and linoleum. Nancy added the family photos, the coffee table covered with cattle-industry publications, the upright piano, and the collection of rusty antique farm implements displayed in the yard.

Cattle work leaves scant time for cooking, and small-scale operations provide little money for household help. A typical ranch breakfast for the children is cereal, eaten in front of the television. The cowgirl and her husband call coffee breakfast most mornings, and it's usually gulped down in the pickup on a feeding

run, or in the barn. At lunchtime it's every cowhand for himself or herself, catch as catch can. Nancy Sheppard, for example, serves lunch at the kitchen counter on paper plates: Steakums on Wonder bread with mayonnaise, fruit salad mixed with pecans and Cool Whip, and Doritos, all washed down with iced tea. For a little variety, Chee-tos make a nice side dish. Or, for a quick Ranch Trailer snack, a heavy hit of aerosol "cheese food" sucked right out of the can sure satisfies. On many ranches Dr. Pepper wins as the daytime beverage of choice. Lone Star or Budweiser beer goes down smooth most evenings once the herd is quiet.

The modern cowgirl wishes her family could all sit down to dinner like the Cleavers on TV or even the way her family did when she was growing up. But with a working mother, working father, and busy kids, the Norman Rockwell meal scene rarely unfolds on today's ranch. Microwave dinners, with each family member doing his or her own nuking, are the order of most days. Sometimes, when the cattle don't require much attention, the cowgirl might fry up some chicken or make her family's favorite chicken-fried steak smothered in thick cream gravy.

The working cowgirl is always hospitable, but she seldom entertains. Occasionally one of the children will have a friend over to spend the night, or a relative will drop in for coffee. But as for sending out invitations, making hors d'oeuvres, and shaking up cocktails—it doesn't happen at the Ranch Trailer. Oh, the cowgirl loves to visit all right, but parties? No way. For one thing, her husband can never seem to find his necktie, and panty hose make her legs itch. Besides, too many people stomping around the mobile home make the rodeo trophies fall off the top of the television set.

The cowgirl's double-wide seems mighty wobbly when compared to the sprawling mansion where Elizabeth Taylor and Rock Hudson lived in the film *Giant*. On television, life at the Ewings' South Fork ranch palace looked pretty tony as well.

At the famous King Ranch they call it the "Big House." A sturdy contrast to the tenuous prefabs, the headquarters of this Southeast Texas cattle empire has been home to four generations of the King-

Kleberg family. A huge adobe dwelling built in 1915, the house sits half a mile from the ranch's main gates. A separate office, pool house, and garages form part of the compound. Even though the arid acreage supports only browned vegetation during portions of the year, a synchronized sprinkler system keeps the lawn and blooming gardens of ranch royalty lush and green at all times. If the King Ranch scene conjures up images of the Benedict family from the novel and movie *Giant*, it should. The Klebergs are said to have inspired that Texas tale.

Two hundred smaller homes dot the King Ranch fiefdom as well. The hired hands, called *kinenos* (a locally coined Tex-Mex word for "King's men") live in them. A few trailers serve hunters leasing parcels of the land, or work as bunkhouses for cowhands riding fences or tending herds in distant pastures. But here too cow folk think of the land itself as home. The Big House seems to sprout right out of the earth, as permanent and solid and sure as the cows, the grass, and the country.

The Big Hacienda—the main house at the King Ranch in Texas.

Mega-ranches like the King Ranch operate as miniature societies, complete with schools and churches and a true sense of community. With hundreds of hired hands and their families in some way dependent on the decisions of the rancher, the solidarity of the Big House becomes an important psychological factor for the people of the ranch. Employees lead their own independent lives, of course. Yet as politically incorrect as it may sound, the mood of a cattle operation is dictated by the timbre of life in the Big House.

I'M GONNA HIRE A COWGIRL TO DECORATE MY HOME

Learning to Love Ponderosa Modern

Want saddles in the bedroom, spurs hanging in the den? Looking for that just-right boot-shaped lamp? A wagonwheel coffee table? How about a sofa with moose-antler armrests? Well, mosey on down to your nearest cowgirl boutique and rustle yourself up some bunkhouse kitsch.

- **Anteks.** 5814 West Lovers Lane, Dallas TX 75225 (214) 528-5567
- **Cowbeaux Collection.** P. O. Box 1702, Santa Fe NM 87504
- **Cry Baby Ranch.** 1422 Larimer Square, Denver CO 80202 (303) 623-3979
- **Raffia**. 10250 Santa Monica Boulevard, Los Angeles CA 90064 (310) 201-0681
- **Rancho**. 322 McKenzie Street, Santa Fe NM 87501 (505) 986-1688.
- **King Ranch Saddle Shop**. 201 East Kleberg, Kingsville TX 78363. (512) 595-5761
- **Guadalupe Hand Prints**. 329 East Ramsey, San Antonio TX 78216. (512) 525-1234
- **Whiskey Dust**. 526 Hudson Street, New York NY 10014 (212) 691-5576
- **Yippie-ei-o!** 7051 East Fifth Avenue, Suite H, Scottsdale AZ 85251. (602) 423-5027.
  Also: 1308 Montana Avenue, Santa Monica CA 90403 (310) 451-2520

- **Deep Texas**. 2173 Portsmouth, Houston TX 77098 (713) 526-2464

How does a ranching family decide where to plant roots on a stretch of country as sprawling and topographically monotonous as the King Ranch? Very practically. New Mexico cattlewoman Virginia Phillips and her husband Chope built a home in 1959 on the northeast corner of their medium-sized spread. Their house, stylish but unpretentious, isn't listed as a National Historic Landmark like the King Ranch behemoth. But amidst the western art and antiques and down-home charm, some mighty elegant ranch living goes on at the Phillips place. The view from the picture window in the breakfast area is panoramic: a dramatic sweep of rolling country sliced by the clean line of a dirt road, the foreground speckled with cows, a pond glistening in the distance. It's a breathtaking vista, but the Phillipses maintain it wasn't the prettiest spot on the property, and aesthetically speaking not their first choice of home sites. They built here because of access to electricity, telephone lines, and the school bus. The Phillips children daily commuted to school sixty-five miles each way.

Silver-haired and regal, Virginia Phillips could be the Prairie Madonna poster girl. She manages her home, cooks for roundup crews, and entertains from time to time, always maintaining an easygoing western nonchalance. She oversees the family's philanthropies too. (Mr. Phillips had a little oil on the side, as in Phillips Petroleum.) Even though she lives fifty miles from the nearest town, and must drive two and a half hours to reach a major airport, Virginia Phillips could hardly be described as provincial. She sees to ranch, family, and personal business in her study, a cozy room with plush carpet and floral upholstery. Recent issues of *Vanity Fair* and *The*

Till Goodan dinnerware.

"Beefmaster" chair by Cathy Boswell.

Guadalupe Hand Prints' "Longhorn" upholstery.

Wall Street Journal spill across an ottoman. Her desk, littered with a modest stack of mail and several sheets of engraved writing paper, looks like a nook to which some proper Victorian lady might retire to catch up on her correspondence. Near the desk hangs a drawing of a weathered old ranch house where the Phillipses once lived. Virginia smiles when she speaks of the years she and her husband shared the shack.

Like the Phillipses, many ranchers eventually abandon the rustic living quarters of previous proprietors for more modern digs. On some spreads, decades-old ranch houses of adobe or stone have somehow come to symbolize poverty and backwardness to the owner. The small operator inherits the land and the livestock, but each new generation abandons the living quarters of the previous one in favor of something more modern. The founders' original headquarters, for instance, might have been left to crumble under a grove of shade trees, when the second generation moved into a ranch-style house nearer the main road. And their children, newlywed and new to the business, might then park mobile homes most anywhere electric lines will reach. On these family spreads, where up-to-date techniques grow high-tech beef, creaky windmills rot above now-dry water wells and decrepit pickups are left to rust in the yard. A rancher's historical perspective varies according to the scope of her holdings.

Like a Marlboro ad, a *Town & Country* magazine spread, or a scene from *Giant*, ranch life as lived by the King Ranch owners or by Virginia and Chope Phillips paints a glamorous picture of cowboy gentility. On a desk in the Phillips living room sits a framed photograph of the couple with their daughter taken at a San Antonio debutante ball. Across the room, a buffalo-hide rug—"We raise a few buffalo here on the ranch"—covers the floor in front of the Phillipses' fireplace. Above the hearth hangs a large lighted painting of a cowboy on horseback pursuing ten or so horses. "A friend painted Chope at work," Virginia explains, "and he really captured the personalities of each of those horses."

Linda and Les Davis, the Phillipses' neighbors, live roughly one hundred miles away. When Linda opens the door and says, "Excuse the mess," it's for good reason. Their nest holds a bit more clutter than the Phillipses'. Why, with all their children and grandchildren and books and hunting trophies and Ping-Pong table and western art and "y'all want some coffee or something?" a modern *Bonanza* episode could be filmed right on the spot. Linda's father, Albert K. Mitchell, was a revered cattleman, western art collector, and agriculture adviser to President Eisenhower. A painting of Mitchell by artist Peter Hurd dominates a wall in one of the original rooms of the Davises' hundred-year-old house. Not far from the Hurd portrait stands a photograph displayed in a Plexiglas frame. Les Davis picks up the photo, a really lovely shot of his daughter and her husband on their wedding day, gazing out over the considerable acreage of the Davises' CS Ranch. Les beams with paternal pride, then he shakes his head and says, "Don't you wish you lived in New Mexico?"

New Mexico, Texas, Colorado, Nevada, wherever. Hanging around the Davis home is enough to make almost anybody fantasize about being head honcha on her very own Rancho Grande. Lots of Americans like to play cowboy and cowgirl. And some like to play at home.

The shoot-'em-up decor of Beth and Jim McCluskey's Arizona ranch house makes the Davis place seem as polished and uptown as a Park Avenue coop: rocking chairs with cowhide upholstery, Indian blankets, cacti all over the place, rough-hewn end tables decorated with brands burned into the wood. Beth's dining-room tabletop saw action as a cattle track in a previous life. Before she served dinner on those boards, cows trod over them to cross a river. A saddle sits on a sawhorse in the den; there's another one in the bedroom. The only thing missing from the McCluskeys' ranch? Cows.

Beth calls the look "cowboy kitsch." Others have dubbed it "cowboyana" or "bunkhouse modern." One collector refers to the style as "neo boy's room," because during the 1950s such buckaroo decor was usually relegated to the bunk-bed-furnished enclaves of Roy Rogers-obsessed little boys. That was before *City Slickers* and Garth Brooks, before grownups started wanting some neat-o cowboy stuff for *their* rooms, not just for their kids'. Cowboy cool is hot. Beth McCluskey should know; she's a designer herself. Through her cow-

GREASE 'N' CHEESE DELUXE

The Truth About Frito Pie: It's Better by the Bag

Fat ingestion the way God intended it—that's the thought behind Frito Pie. There are plenty of wrong ways to make it. Using vegetarian chili kills the mood. So do "lite" chips. And those nouvelle southwestern cuisine places that experiment by putting goat cheese or Gorgonzola on this cowboy casserole—well, it's a sacrilege.

The building blocks of the perfect Frito Pie are Fritos (the small ones), chili (either homemade or canned without beans), cheese (grated cheddar only, please), chopped onions, and jalapeño peppers.

In Austin at the Texas Chili Parlor, they do it this way: Fritos in a bowl. Chili—either the sissy one-X, more macho two-X, or scalding three-X caliber—goes over the chips. Cheese is sprinkled over the chili. Onions and jalapeños and saltines are served on the side.

To really experience the caloric, indigestion-causing splendor of this southwestern classic, eat it at any county fair, rodeo, or buffalo-chip-throwing contest west of the Mississippi. There, the Knights of Columbus, or the Ladies' Garden Club, or the Policemen's Benevolent League will likely present the cowboy ambros ia thusly: Neatly cut open a lunch-box-sized bag of Fritos. Pour in some warm canned chili. Add cheese. Charge $1.25, including a napkin and a plastic spoon.

They bag it in Manhattan also, at the Cowgirl Hall of Fame Barbecue. There, the Frito bag is put on a plate, cut open, and folded back to make room for the chili, cheese, onion, and a dollop of sour cream. The forks aren't plastic, and the price tag isn't $1.25, but the heartburn is just as good.

boy-chic shops, she's turning other city slickers on to the joys of the Ponderosa life.

Western collectibles and cowboy-decor shops are spread throughout America. Who's buying all this stuff? Cowgirlish designer Barbara Cooper of Santa Fe describes the cowboy-kitsch connoisseurs who visit her store as varied, a few ranchers and lots of urbanites browsing for campy bits of the Old West.

Don't look for any cowboy collectibles in Rebecca Gonzales's trailer. You won't find much of it at Virginia Phillips's place either. Urban cowgirls decorate with chaps and spurs, real cowgirls wear them. Former TV anchorwoman Linda Ellerbee displays old cowboy boots as objets d'art in her home. Faith Popcorn—author of *The Popcorn Report*—believes she must have seen action as a cowgirl in a former life. Maybe so; her cottage on Long Island would blend into the Montana landscape just fine. Filled with saddles, Native American paraphernalia, and bleached steer skulls, the place more than makes up for all the Lone Ranger bedspreads and cowboy lamps Faith never had as a child.

Anna Lively, an aspiring Los Angeles actress, does cowboy kitsch one better. She decorates with cows. There's a cow on the welcome mat in the hallway outside her penthouse. A spotted cowhide rug is on the apartment floor. Cow magnets on the refrigerator. Cow coffee cups. Cow light switches. Cow-print throw pillows. A cuddly stuffed cow toy lounges on the waterbed. More cows loll at Anna's than at most working ranches.

The trend doesn't stop with cutesy cows or covered-wagon-shaped lamps, either. Furniture by Thomas Molesworth, the trail boss of cowboy design, brings top dollar at antique shows and auctions. Molesworth worked in Wyoming during the 1930s. His pieces sold briskly for a few decades, ultimately forcing major furniture manufactures to follow with their own mass-produced western lines. Until recently, the market for the work of Thomas Molesworth hibernated, and only the most academic collectors ventured out to buy. Then, not long ago, the Buffalo Bill Historical Society sponsored a traveling exhibition of Molesworth furniture—and suddenly the rush was on.

Today a collector hoping to snag a Molesworth original must search long and hard. The reported asking price recently for a Molesworth sofa was $18,000. A buyer actually parted with $20,000 for a Molesworth dining-room set. Not too surprisingly, a herd of imitators have taken up the trail, stepping into the master's boots. A few of these neo-Molesworths are designing women. Albuquerque cowgirl Susan Kirkpatrick customizes her ranch-style furniture with decorative bronc-rider motifs and hand-forged drawer pulls in the shape of steer heads. Texas furniture maker Cathy Boswell sums up her cowboy-inspired "Beefmaster" chairs—with bones from a bovine rib cage forming the back slats, and spotted hide for the seat upholstry—as "Molesworth on acid."

Not all converts to the cowboy movement get into the furniture. Some stick with the authentic Old West artifacts such as spurs and saddles and branding irons. Others go for textiles—almost anything with fringe. Antique bedspreads and those silly souvenir tablecloths once sold in highway curio stands like Stuckey's have been resurrected as art objects costing hundreds of dollars. Beth McCluskey saw an old "Welcome to Arizona" bandanna framed in a customer's den. "And it looked terrific."

Ranchers love to emblazon their brand on everything from cows to luggage to guest towels. A San Antonio fabric company, Guadalupe Hand Prints, got started by exploiting that decorative quirk. The company's chief designer didn't stop with Double Bar Rs and Lazy Ws. Today her line of prickly-pear prints, barbed-wire designs, and spurs and saddles cover the sofas, windows, walls, and sometimes even the backs of city folk who never dreamed of owning a livestock brand.

Then there's the dinnerware bonanza. When serving supper on a cowboy tablecloth, you might as well put out your best Westward Ho! china. The late artist Till Goodan drew the old Gene Autry comic strips and designed the movie cowboy's personal Christmas cards. Goodan took the cowboy aesthetic to dinner during the 1950s with his dinnerware designs. When a hundred-piece set of Goodan bowls and plates and cups sold for $4,000 a few years ago, the artist's daughter decided it was time to relicense Dad's old patterns. Now a whole new generation of little buckaroos is slurping through their cornflakes to find the cowboy at the bottom of the bowl.

So you've got your Molesworth-style chairs around your antique cattle-track dining table. A vintage Hopalong Cassidy bedspread works fine as a tablecloth, and each place is set with cow camp-china. What do you serve? Cowboy chow. Chili, barbecue, chicken-fried steak. No tofu, no tabouli. Meat, meat, and more meat. And maybe some beans. Beef is real food, remember? And it's not just the cowgirl's vocation; it's also her breakfast, lunch, and dinner.

On many corporate cattle operations, the chuck wagon has been replaced with the caterer's truck. But the same items hit the spot on all ranches, corporate or family owned. A cook who turns out nice biscuits gets high marks from a cattle crew, and a stout cup of cowboy coffee is savored like fine wine.

Sherry Delamarter grew up in Fort Worth, practically weaned on barbecue and chili and hot biscuits. When she left Texas to seek fame and fortune in New York City, Sherry felt homesick for Cowtown cooking. So she opened up a restaurant dedicated to the spirit of the cattlewoman's table, called the Cowgirl Hall of Fame Barbecue. Employees answer the phone simply, "Cowgirl." In addition to Los Angeles, Houston, and other U.S. cities, Delamarter has plans for a Cowgirl Hall of Fame Barbecue in Taiwan and other parts of Asia as well. She believes it's unfair to the rest of the world to keep southern hospitality strictly below the Mason-Dixon Line.

"New York City? Get a rope!" In what has to be one of the wildest ironies this side of a picante-sauce commercial, the Cowgirl Hall of Fame restaurant of Manhattan has actually been hired to cater barbecues in cattle country. Big-time ranch hostesses will go all out when it comes to a fiesta, even if it means airlifting in meat from you-know-where. Lots of cattlewomen opt to have their large get-togethers professionally planned and executed. Others rely on their own crack crew of kitchen help and ranch hands to fire up the big mesquite pits, mix up the secret sauce, and spice the

THE COWGIRL POET

Coming Home

By Laurie Wagner Buyer

Horses hock deep in snow, miles
steaming from slick hides, bareback
on the appy, he pulls
the saddled paint behind.

The road ends here, where
mail stops, where plows
turn back for town, where
I wait in mid-day quiet.

Solitude ends here, beyond
the constant touch of other lives,
the beginning of the world, lodgepole,
willow and the river.

I am grateful the horses come, ears
perked in curious greeting, grateful
only his eyes speak, snow mingled in
graying hair he reaches out, packs me
close to damp warmth,
takes me home.

beans. Some guests arrive by helicopter; others stay the night. Ranchers take revelry seriously, and extravagance is more rule than exception.

Fern Sawyer used to put on the hog for guests at her ranch in New Mexico. It seems Fern likes to rest a spell between blowouts— her last big shindig honored Jack Kennedy in 1962. "That was one hell of a party. We served barbecue to three thousand people. Lyndon and Lady Bird were here," she says matter-of-factly. "It got wild. All those crazy Democrats. But you know the only thing they stole was one towel from the guest bathroom. That was a long time ago. Politicians nowadays are liable to take off with the piano or a couple of calves."

Whether offering coffee to friends or arranging slow-cooked sides of beef for a few hundred, cowgirls and cattlewomen know a thing or two about southwestern hospitality. Be it bologna sandwiches served on paper plates, or filet mignon presented on china with the ranch brand, any meal proffered in cattle country will satisfy. Charles Russell originals or sofa-sized nature prints from local starving-artist sales—no matter what the value of her art collection, a cowgirl's home always feels cozy. There might be a *New York Times* folded on the nightstand at some ranch headquarters. At other outfits, bedtime headlines lean more toward "I AM THE LOVE-CHILD OF ELVIS AND BIGFOOT." Whether a house has served the family for generations or has just been put up on blocks, whether begonias bloom in the yard or an abandoned washing machine rusts there, inside every ranch-house door hangs a rack laden with ropes and tack and Stetsons. And at both the Ranch Trailer and the Big Hacienda visitors are as welcome as sunshine, as long as they can excuse the mess.

CHAPTER FOUR

RANCH ROMANCE

MIDDLE-AGED BACHELOR SOUGHT. Prosperous 130-pound lady rancher with a full head of hair, keen eyes, and no false teeth desires life companion. The lady enjoys indoor and outdoor activities, and holds deeds to property valued at $10,000. Dudes need not apply.

THIS NO-NONSENSE cowgirl personal ad placed by Miss Ellen Callahan in an 1887 edition of *Hoof and Horn* issued a call for one good man. Think times have changed? Maybe, but consider this item from the classified pages of a Texas newspaper not long ago: *Calling cute cowboys! SWF seeks stud in ropers and Wranglers. I enjoy two-stepping, country music ...*

It's the same old story,

MY VALENTINE
I hope to lasso your heart.

this version set against a backdrop of cacti and cattle. Cowgirl seeks cowboy. And vice versa. The honest cowgirl will tell you flat out that cows and courage aren't all that count. A sense of family looms large in the westerner's heart too. And no matter how intimidating her swagger or how cocky her talk, there are some things even the most competent cowgirl cannot accomplish on her own.

Perhaps the cowgirl's nesting instinct relates somehow to her relationship with fertile land and fecund livestock, and her proximity to the cycles of nature. Could be that matrimonial and maternal urges creep up on the cowgirl in much the same way a premonition of a coming rain might overtake her.

63

Or maybe she espouses the basic family values of rural America, plain and simple. Then again, perhaps the cowgirl doesn't differ much from other women in this respect. She gets lonely. She hears the tick, tick, ticking of the biological clock. And that just-right cowboy comes along, tips his hat, says "howdy" and sweeps her off her feet. Or maybe she sweeps him off his feet. At any rate, not only do cowgirls and cowboys need each other for the obvious reasons, camping under the stars approaches new frontiers in fun when using a sleeping bag built for two. Married cowgirls agree: There's nothing quite like ranching with the one you love.

The cowgirl's horizon, typically, seems a panorama of hide, horn, and hunks. Beef and beefcake. Well, O.K., maybe not always hunks and beefcake, but the cowgirl's life usually comes heavily populated with men of various ages, shapes, sizes, and dispositions. Naturally, most women have fathers and brothers and male co-workers, but cattle tending provides a unique opportunity for platonic male-female relationships. There's no time for coquettishness when hog-tying a steer. No time for guys' macho posturing either. From the cowgirl's professional perspective, men are partners, friends, equals. But when it comes to matters of the heart—sometimes just the jingle of a certain cowboy's spurs can make even the most pragmatic cowgirl go cow-eyed.

For generations cowboys have tended to portray women in bovine terms. Cowgirls draw such comparisons, too, perhaps likening a handsome man to a bull worthy of separating from the herd and branding as her own. To suggest an analogy between a cowboy and a prized breeder isn't a slur—at least not against the cowboy. If it smells sexist, consider for a moment the high regard in which the cowpoke holds quality livestock.

Singers of one old song, for example, drawled this cowboy couplet describing a lady: *"She ranges in the Live Oak branch:/The purtiest heifer at the ranch."* No doubt the guy who dreamed up the poetic personification of his girl as a top-grade beef cow meant the words to melt his beloved's heart, or at least to convey to fellow cowpokes the high esteem in which he held her. Frontiersmen often became sort of myopic when talk turned sweet; they couldn't see past their own wild environs.

Davy Crockett was well known for his colorful descriptions of womenfolk. The uniquely eloquent Crockett painted one female acquaintance as being able to "sing a wolf to sleep." Another could "laugh the bark off a pine tree." In an attempt to compliment a woman bereft of musical talent, Crockett tossed this consolation

IS HIS NECK *TOO* RED?

A Quiz

Is he a cowboy dilettante or a redneck clod? You know he's a cracker if . . .

- His richest relative buys a new home and he has to help take the wheels off.
- His mother doesn't remove the cigarette from her lips when telling the cop to "kiss my ass."
- Directions to his house include "turn off the paved road."
- His sister's hairdo has ever been ruined by a ceiling fan.
- His mother keeps a spit cup on the ironing board.
- He has a rag for a gas cap.
- He thinks Vienna sausage on a saltine is an hors d'oeuvre.
- There is a stuffed possum mounted in his home.
- He considers a can of beer and bug zapper quality entertainment.
- The primary color of his car is Bondo.

- He truly believes that women are turned on by animal noises and tongue gestures.
- His family tree does not fork.
- He has barbecued Spam on the grill.
- He regularly uses "party" as a verb.
- His favorite movies star that "Ernest" guy.
- The diploma in his den includes the words "Trucking Institute."
- "What are you lookin' at, Butthead?" is the most common phrase uttered at his family reunion.
- He has at times been too drunk to fish.
- His brothers are named Larry Wayne, Junior, and Bubba.
- He believes the Styrofoam beer cooler to be the greatest invention of all time.
- In all photos of him there's a toothpick in his mouth.

praise: She could "outscream a catamount and jump over her own shadow" and she "knew a woodchuck from a skunk." Sweet, huh?

Early songs, poems, and legends of the Old West indicate that cowboys and other frontiersmen seemed to have mentally herded women into three distinct corrals. First there were the "true ladies." Idealized womanhood, dainty, frilly, loyal, and fair with a quiet inner

strength, these were the girls lonesome cowhands dreamed of marrying. Then there were the "sporting women." Prostitutes, showgirls, and other stout-hearted businesswomen trafficking in carnal goods, these were the gals trail-weary cowhands dreamed of bedding down. Finally came the cowgirls, or "backwoods belles." Strong, confident, daring, these women possessed many of the same qualities the cowboys prided themselves on having. And while men of the Old West may have fantasized about marrying a true lady, or tingled at the thought of a roll in the hay with a sporting woman, the cowgirl was his friend, co-worker and often his life mate.

What the women of the Old West found attractive in men is more difficult to say. There's no wealth of cow*girl* songs lending insight into exactly what the pioneer woman deemed dreamboatish. Tight jeans? Good manners? Wit? Maybe. But it's more probable that in the days before the West was tamed, a woman concentrated on a few important must-have characteristics when searching for a spouse: Good hygiene. Kindness. Trustworthiness. Physical strength and stamina. If her chosen one just so happened to be a face jock, good dancer, and handy around the house, then she'd struck matrimonial gold.

These days, a cowgirl shopping the man market can afford to be choosy. Kindness and honesty are musts. But brawn, once considered a necessity on the plains, rates as no more than a nice perk in a 1990s husband. In the cowgirl's quest for a potential mate nowadays, a sense of humor, intelligence, and social grace have become much more valued attributes than, say, good horsemanship. As ranching has lurched with fits and starts into the twentieth century, so has ranch romance.

Although they frequently embrace the institution of marriage, cowgirls by nature are not joiners or subscribers. Many see themselves as independent, neither Democrat nor Republican, mavericks riding outside the system. "Never had any need for it," forms a cowhand's standard evaluation of everything from yoga to Cuisinart to *Roe* v. *Wade*. It should come as no shock that the Women's Movement and the Men's Movement never really caught on down on the ranch.

Talk of sex, relationships, and gender roles is mighty scarce chitchat around the cattlewoman's table, unless the subjects of the conversation happen to be cows.

"I don't believe in all that bra-burning women's-lib stuff," many a cowgirl has said. And why should she? The cowgirl has long epitomized female professionalism and financial independence. She has demanded and received equal treatment in a male-dominated field for generations—assuming her ability warrants it. The cowgirl endorses, almost rabidly, the notion of fair compensation for work well done. Yet she shies away from the term "feminist." Blame it on stubbornness, or unwillingness to rock the boat any more than she already has with her life choices. Or maybe it's simply a "you take care of your business and I'll take care of mine" attitude that prevents the cowgirl from taking up the banner and championing the feminist cause.

Male bonding and healing the inner child haven't really caused much of a stir in cowboy circles either. The cowboy has long been a fairly liberated, sensitive man, whether he cares to admit it or not. Despite the image of the cowpoke as one tough piece of gristle, today's ranchman seems more Alan Alda than John Wayne. He tends to assume a

A WEAKNESS FOR COWBOYS

The Cowgirl's Male-Order Wish List

- Roy Rogers
- Gary Cooper
- The Marlboro Man
- Cowboy Curtis from *Pee-Wee's Playhouse*
- Nolan Ryan
- Clint Black
- Louis L'Amour
- John Wayne
- Paul Newman as "Hud"
- Ross Perot
- Sam Shepard

- Riders in the Sky
- Waddie Mitchell
- Ted Turner
- Chuck Yeager
- Jesse Jackson
- Yosemite Sam
- Robert Duvall
- Larry McMurtry
- John Connolly
- Rock Hudson in *Giant*
- Ty Murray
- Will Rogers
- Howdy Doody
- Kris Kristofferson

- Thomas McGuane
- Bob Wills & The Texas Playboys
- Michael Martin Murphy
- Dan Jenkins
- Denzel Washington
- Robert Redford
- Larry Mahan
- Don Edwards
- General Norman Schwarzkopf
- Larry Mahan
- Lyle Lovett

larger role at home than his urban counterpart does. The cowboy will sometimes pack his children along while he works. And he's as proud of his culinary skills as he is of his prowess on horseback. He's Mr. Mom, the Galloping Gourmet, and the Lone Ranger all rolled into one amazing man.

The Crosbys, who ranched in New Mexico at the turn of the century, illustrated how beef growing has long been a family affair. After the birth of a daughter, Mr. Crosby, bottle in one pocket and diapers in the other, would ride the range with the infant nestled in the saddle in front of him. When he needed to dismount to mend a fence or doctor a calf, he'd pass the little girl to his wife, also on horseback. Every few hours the Crosbys would take a break to feed the baby, and if they found a fresh cow they could replenish the bottle without riding all the way back to the house. It was sort of the Old West equivalent of child care in the workplace.

Rebecca Gonzales's husband, Richard, takes his infant daughter to the barn with him. He pushes her stroller into a shady spot, and gets busy helping another man shoe one of their horses, a small gray filly. Every few minutes, every few seconds really, Richard stops what he's doing to check the baby. "This is her horse," he

Rodeo star Tad Lucas with daughter Mitzi.

ALL HAT AND NO CATTLE

"Howdy, honey" Gone High Tech

Cowboys these days craft some creative and mighty racy come-ons when trying to herd a human heifer home from the honky-tonk. These down-home double entendres aren't recommended reading for those who blush easily.

- I'm writing a book about the best pickup lines in America. Which one works best on you?

- Why don't you let me buy you a double. By the time you finish it, you'll think I'm Clint Black.

- NON-VERBAL COWBOY COME-ON #1: Eye contact.

- I'll bet you a beer that I can tell you where you got those boots . . . You got them on your feet!

- NON-VERBAL COWBOY COME-ON #2: Raising a beer bottle in a toast.

- Look at that! You're so hot you made my ice cubes melt.

- GUY: Hey, you look like you might have a little cowboy in ya'? . . .
  GAL: Not really . . .
  GUY: Well, would you like to have?

- Have you ever ridden a bull? . . . Would you like to tonight?

- I've been to three rodeos and a buzzard orgy, but you're just about the most excitin' thing I've ever seen.

- NON-VERBAL COWBOY COME-ON #3: Licking the lips, making animal sounds, and moving the pelvis in a lewd manner.

says, glancing in the direction of the pink bundle squirming in the stroller. The cowboy father then turns his voice to baby talk; kneeling before his tiny daughter, he coos, "This is your horse. Yes, it is. This is my girl's horse. This is my girl's horse." The little girl thinks this very funny. She smiles and gurgles at her dad, and then looks intently at the horse, her horse. If she could talk, she'd probably tell daddy to cut the baby babble and get back to work. In just a couple of years this cowgirl will be ready to ride.

Here's a ranch romance, a cowgirl love scene—of sorts: Vera McGinnis didn't resort to fisticuffs with the intention of impressing her man, but she certainly didn't mind his witnessing her triumph. It seems that a stable boy had saddled another cowgirl's favorite horse for Vera to ride. This apparently did not sit well with the other cowgirl. Unkind words flew, and finally Vera shed her spurs and prepared to pop open a can of kickass. The two women exchanged blows and pinches and bites while the other cowboys and cowgirls cheered them on. "Twist her ear!" they shouted to neither woman in particular. Finally, like sweet music, Vera heard the voice of her boyfriend hollering, "'Atta baby, sock her!" Inspired by her beloved's encouragement, Vera rallied, clobbering her opponent with a decisive bite, hair pull, and scissor hold. But wait, here's the really romantic part: When it was all over, Vera's beau led his battle-weary sweetheart away and lovingly poulticed her black eye with meat.

Not all cowgirl courtships progress like plots of action-adventure movies. Virginia and Chope Phillips first came together calmly, in Amarillo, when he was dating her roommate during World War II. A horse brought cowgirl Cindy Price and her husband, Will, together, when, as just a little girl, she bought a colt from him. Rebecca Gonzales remembers the first time she laid eyes on Richard at a local rodeo. She was twelve, he was twenty, and she got angry when he teased her about her barrel-racing technique.

Linda Davis knew Les to be the one and only cowboy for her from the first time she saw him too. It took Les a little longer to come around. As a young fellow fresh out of Dartmouth University, he stopped by her father's ranch to talk business. Linda thought him

dashing and sophisticated; he figured her as just another cute kid. But the cute kid grew into a knockout young woman, and when Les met Linda a second time, five years later, he fell, smitten by her cowgirlish charms.

Some cautious cowgirls like to ease into commitment slowly. Dale Evans first tipped her hat to Roy Rogers at Edwards Air Force Base in California, where he was performing. Dale remembers, "No skyrockets went off; no bells rang. Roy Rogers seemed to me to be a rather shy, mannerly cowboy with reasonably good looks and a nice singing voice. Nothing more, nothing less." Later, after she and Roy become friends, and had worked together in many movies, Dale Evans changed her mind. In 1947, she and the mannerly cowboy swapped "I dos."

Texas rancher Lady Bird Johnson didn't hurry to the altar either. She first encountered her husband, the late president, in Austin when she was a recent college graduate and he was a congressional aide. He asked her to marry him on their very first date. Even though she recalled having a "queer moth-in-the-flame feeling about the remarkable young man," it took three months of courtship and convincing before Lady Bird finally agreed to take the plunge.

Going up to the Dairy Queen in the pickup truck to get a Coca-Cola. Catching a picture show. Smooching on the front porch. Stepping out to a honky-tonk to slide a two-step around a sand-sprinkled dance floor. Cow-couple courtship usually progresses along a pretty predictable line. The western-style marriage proposal, on the other hand, can be a cow of a different color.

Cowboys don't pull diamond engagement rings out of thin air, you know. Just ask Jill Smith. A Dallas girl with no ranching in her background, it took Jill awhile to catch the rhythm of the range. She knew she was making progress the day her ranchman boyfriend invited her to go check on some cows. They bounced over dirt roads to a remote area of the ranch, where a recent rain had turned a grazing area into a field of mud. Jill's boyfriend explained that the bog could present a problem for the herd and suggested they investigate, see how deep it might be. Reluctantly, Jill pulled on a pair of waist-high rubber boots, and followed her favorite cowboy into the quag-

THE COWGIRL POET

Cowgirling After Motherhood

By Kay Kelley

You know, before our little son was born
In utter bliss I would ride the range
Helping rancher friends gather their cattle
And never thinking that things would change.

For I just loved that cowboy way of life
And the savvy to get the work done.
Long hours or bad weather never dampened
A job that I considered pure fun.

Life takes a turn after a child arrives
For a mom is "on call" day and night.
Now when I get a chance to ride I find
I view it in a different light.

In spring, when the pasture's littered with calves
And each one bucks and plays like a clown,
While mothering hormones course through my veins,
Bawling calves can make my milk let down.

It never bothered me how slow they drove
When we found a bunch on the backside,
Or waiting while hands cleaned out the corners,
Up riding point—I enjoyed the ride.

Now I'm pushing drag—riding back and forth.
You see the pressure is getting worse.
My supportive hubby waits at the pens
He's got a baby that needs to nurse.

The brandings were always a special time
We looked forward to every year.
As a part of the team—caught up in the work,
I'd turn each bull calf into a steer.

But now, all of the calves look like BABIES!
And I'm more attuned to how they feel.
I continue to brand and cut and mark
But I'm lacking my previous zeal.

There's this uncontrollable urge I get
That just might get me shot because
When the shipping calves are cut and sorted,
I want to turn them in with their mas.

And so I wrestle with these new feelings
And watch our son who's approaching two.
Though I'm missing some works—my time's well-spent
Raising our littlest buckaroo.

mire. The ooze slid up to her knees, then toward her thighs and Jill felt a dull pang of nostalgia for city life. *What am I doing here in this mud hole with this yahoo? Ah, for a man in a necktie and smelling of aftershave!* Just as she began plodding back toward solid land, giving up on cowboys for good, he stopped her. "Hey, what's this?" he yelled, digging around in the slime. Curious, Jill reached gingerly into the muck near where he dug. She felt around for a moment until her fingers wrapped around a small, hard square—a box? Inside, she found a one-and-a-half-carat diamond ring. Knee-deep in odiferous mud, the cowboy asked her to marry him. He'd even iced down a bottle of Dom Perignon in the bushes nearby. Jill says the whole scene was witnessed by seven cows, mooing and shaking their heads as if to say, "Humans! Go figure."

As unconventional as their moment of betrothal, Jill and Bragg Smith wed in a traditional ceremony in a Dallas church followed by a barbecue reception at the ranch. Other cowgirls opt for something a bit more showy when it comes to those sacred vows, often dumping a lifetime of creative entertainment ideas into a single affair.

An Oklahoma couple, children of neighboring ranches, tied the knot several years ago in what has to be the quintessential cowgirl wedding. The bride wore white. Her attendants donned bright dotted-swiss formals, each girl bedecked in a different rainbow color—pink, lavender, mint green. The groom sported stiffly starched denim jeans, cowboy boots, a cowboy hat, and a white dinner jacket. His supporters dressed in the same ensemble, except their cummerbunds and bow ties matched their boots *and* corresponded in color to one of the bridesmaids' dresses. The ceremony unfolded in the traditional way: "Do you take, blah, blah, blah . . . ." Once the couple had kissed however, the bride turned toward the congregation, gathered her skirt and train, took the microphone from its stand, and right then and there belted out every single verse of "I Was Country When Country Wasn't Cool."

Some cowgirls like to get married on horseback. Bride and bridegroom trot up to a mounted man of the cloth, and from the saddle promise to love, honor, and cherish. Other brides use the horse as bridesmaid. Andrea Baker doesn't think of herself as a cowgirl, but she married her husband, Nash, in a field of wildflowers with Buck the Wonder Horse as a witness. Sometimes a rodeo arena makes a nice venue for a cowgirl sacrament. For a mid-rodeo ceremony, squeezed in between the bull riding and the greased pig chase, one bride wound a wreath of baby's breath around her cowboy hat and carried a bucket of daisies as a bouquet.

THE BUCKLE BUNNY HOP

Like Rabbits on the Rodeo Road

If you've ever seen those birds perched on cows' backs or noticed on National Geographic the little fish swimming around beneath sharks, you know something about buckle bunnies—the groupies of men's pro rodeo. A gaggle of chicks, not rabbits, these gals' goal is to unfasten a cowboy's championship belt buckle and take him for a ride around the bedroom he'll never forget.

World Champion All-Around Cowboy Ty Murray and many of the other handsome athletes on the circuit are single. And many of the married cowboys travel without their wives. Enter the buckle bunnies. These gals follow the rodeo at their own expense. They request airplane seating near their bull-riding prey. They stay in the hotels where the cowboys bunk, and stalk their quarry from breakfast to bedtime and beyond. They do the fellows' laundry, run errands, apply balm to sore muscles, and see to a cowboy's most personal needs.

While the buckle bunnies flirt, coo, and cajole, the cowboys' steady girlfriends and wives polish their rabbit punches. The bunny brigade has prompted more than one rodeo wife to stay at her husband's side on the road, and prompted still others to file for divorce.

Some guys like the attention. But others see the bunnies as a blight. "They're downright pesky," one bull rider says. "You can't get away from them. After one rough ride, who wants another?"

FOUR STEPS TO THE PERFECT TWO-STEP

A Lesson for Beginners

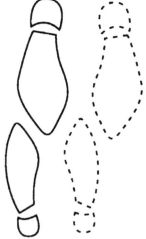

Right

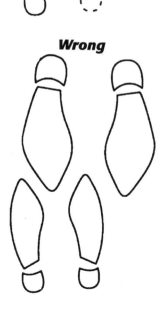

Wrong

Cowgirling is hard to fake in the rodeo arena. But it's easy on the dance floor. Even gals who can't ride a bronc or rope a calf can slide a two-step. Here's how.

1. Grab a cowboy. Your left hand on his right shoulder, your right hand holding his left.
2. Step the left foot foward—count 1, slow.
3. Step the right foot beside the left—count 2, slow.
4. Step left foot forward—count 3 quick. Step feet together—count 4, quick.

An easy way to remember: Slow, slow, quick, quick.

When the children of two ranch families tied the knot in Arizona not long ago, they spared no extravagance. First, helped by their wedding consultant, they issued invitations engraved with their new cattle brand. At the altar, the wedding party wore Old West evening attire. Following the ceremony, the same brand—a symbol of the young folk's new union—was burned into each and every steak served at the reception. These two said, "I love you," not with flowers, but with meat.

So what happens once the wedding guests have gone and all the thank-you notes are mailed? The cowgirl concentrates her energies on marriage—when she's not too busy with the herd and ranch chores. A Mrs. Stevens ranched in Lonesome Valley, Arizona, during the wild days of the Old West. With her husband away one day, Mrs. Stevens and her children were besieged by Apaches. Alone, she kept the unfriendly warriors at bay with gunfire until a band of well-armed cowboys happened by, shooing the invaders away. Before leaving, the cowboys asked if Mrs. Stevens would like to send a message to her husband. She wrote:

Dear Lewis,
The Apaches came. I'm mighty nigh out of buckshot.
Please send more. Your loving wife.

A good partnership forms only part of the cowgirl-cowboy marital equation. Humor and fun figure into the mix as well. Or at least Dale Evans thinks so. A recent visitor to the Roy Rogers and Dale Evans Museum commented to Dale about how handsome Roy still is and how much current country-music heartthrob Clint Black favors him. Dale looked at Roy for a second, and then replied, "He is cute, isn't he? And you know what? He's just a whole lot of fun."

Any marital advice issued by Dale Evans or Roy Rogers merits heeding. Wed for more than forty years now, the parents of nine children, sixteen grandchildren, twenty-five and counting great-grandchildren, Dale and Roy seem the ideal couple, partners who work together, play together, and pray together even if they're not always physically side by side. When Dale's father passed away, a contractual obligation prevented Roy from accompanying her to the funeral.

"You don't have to *go* with me to *be* with me, you know," Dale told him. A bond like the Rogerses' doesn't hinge on constant contact; it's a mental, emotional, spiritual thing.

Other cowgirls don't always have it so good. Sometimes even the sweetest unions turn sour. Firm believers in "if it ain't broke don't fix it," cow couples often fail to heed the knocks and rattles indicating that the marital machinery needs a tune-up. Still, cowgirl tenacity applies to marriage, as well as to ranch chores. When a cowgirl falls off, she climbs right back on again, usually sticking with a job until she either gets it right or gets tired of trying. Lucille Mulhall married twice. So did Fern Sawyer, who remained friends with both her exes.

Legendary cowgirl Sally Skull married repeatedly. Rebecca Gonzales married the same man twice. Calamity Jane never got hitched. Hallie Stillwell and Lady Bird Johnson were left widows their first and only times out of the chute. Even Dale Evans had heard "The Bridal Chorus" twice before it rang just right with Roy.

To the cowgirl's way of thinking, marriage is a lot like riding bucking stock. You hope you get it right the first time, but if you don't, you dust yourself off and try again. With luck, you won't make the same mistake twice.

During branding, mother cows go to one pen and calves to another. This separation creates a terrible racket, all the bovine babies bawling for their mamas, and all the mamas calling out for their offspring. Finally, once the last horns have been tipped, and the branding irons begin to cool, the mother cows and their little ones reunite in a scene that's not unlike what happens when the bell rings at kindergarten and all the noisy kids run directly to the right station wagon with the right mommy at the wheel. Cowgirls call this "mothering up" when it's done at the ranch with cows. When it takes place at kindergarten, it's just called "car pool."

Cows make good mothers, and cowgirls follow their example. Dale Evans was once honored as California's Mother of the Year. She and Roy adopted children at quite a clip. The Rogers clan grew at such a rate that Dale once told Roy, "We are either going to have to stop visiting orphanages, or buy us a hotel to live in." They did neither. Instead, they just opened their arms wider to embrace each new son or daughter.

In addition to liberal doses of the obvious—love, affection, guidance—the secret to successful child rearing on the prairie is to instill in kids a love of the land and a respect for animals, rules of safety around the equipment, and most importantly, the ability to ride horseback. Some variation on the prodigious equestrienne story is offered up on almost every ranch. "I was riding by the time I was eight," one cowgirl boasts. Another gal bests that easily, insisting, "Oh, I did my first riding trick at age six." As a child, Lucille Mulhall preferred horses to dolls. A tyro horsewoman at age two, little Lucille

cried to get on the horse and wailed even louder when time came to get off. The intent of all this ride 'em toddler stuff is to produce ranch children capable of handling the unexpected.

Idella Smyers perhaps took this theory a bit too far. She ranched in Texas long ago and was known to be rough on cows and children, although thoroughly devoted to both. Idella awarded each of her offspring a horse of his or her very own—an unbroken horse, to keep only if the child could tame it. She also bathed her big brood by running them through the cattle tank. Perhaps she even fed the kids cattle cake when times were lean. No doubt the junior members of the Smyers clan figured fast how to handle raw deals in rough territory.

Often the cowgirl concentrating on mothering finds it difficult to quit thinking about cows. When pioneer cowgirl Asenath Alkire was expecting her first baby, she went away from the ranch to stay with relatives and be near a doctor. A few days after her departure, her husband received word that a telegram awaited him in town. Delighted at the prospect of seeing his wife and newborn, Mr. Alkire

A BETTER CLASS OF LOSER

Where to find a cold longneck, a two-step, and a roomful of urban cowboys.

- **Billy Bob's**. 2520 Rodeo Plaza, Fort Worth TX 76106. (817) 624-7117.
- **Branson, Missouri**. The entire town.
- **Denim & Diamonds**. 32000 Ocean Park, Santa Monica CA 90405. (310) 452-3446.
- **The Cocky Bull**. 14180 Highway 395, Victorville CA 92392. (619) 241-2855.
- **Gerry Andal's Ranch**. 620 Southeast Everett Mall Way, Everett WA 98204. (206) 355-7999.
- **Gruene Hall**. 1281 Gruene Road, New Braunfels TX 78130. (512) 625-0142.
- **The Lone Star Roadhouse**. 240 West 52nd Street, New York NY 10019. (212) 245-2950.
- **The Million Dollar Cowboy Bar**. 25 North Cache, Jackson Hole WY 83001. (307) 733-2207.
- **The Rose**. 6363 Richmond, Houston TX 77057. (713) 978-7673.
- **Toolie's Country**. 4231 West Thomas, Phoenix AZ 85019. (602) 233-0210.

3449-10

Cowboy
and
Cowgirl
CUT-OUTS

packed and prepared to travel, first to the telegraph office and then on to the bedside of his wife and child. Imagine his disappointment when he read the wire from Asenath: "Can you furnish three hundred fat steers? What price?"

BARNYARD BALLET

The Advanced Curriculum

The two-step is the see-Spot-run first lesson of country dancing. The true cowgirl Ginger Rogers goes for more exotic choreography.

- The Tush Push
- The Electric Slide
- The Birdy Dance
- The Slappin' Leather
- The Achy Breaky Heart
- The Swamp Rat
- The Whiskey Wiggle
- The Tomato Patch Shuffle
- The Shorthorn Boogie
- The Bar-None Strut

- The Cowboy Cha-Cha
- Ten Pretty Girls
- The Kickin' Trouble
- The Six-Pack
- The Alley Cat
- The Lover's Lariat
- The Double Eagle
- The Across-Texas Waltz
- The Dirty Leg
- The Ruthie

Some children are born bowlegged and take to ranch life naturally. Others never shine to roping and riding at all. All six of Linda and Les Davis's children seemed natural-born cowhands from day one; today each of them remains involved in some aspect of the family's CS Ranch. Neither the son nor daughter of Chope and Virginia Phillips heard the calling, although they both have fond memories of growing up on the ranch. Cowgirls and cowboys understand that not every child is cut out to take over the reins of a family business. There's little sense in pushing a budding pianist to become a cattleman. If the boot fits, however, most ranching moms and dads are tickled to teach a son or daughter the ropes. Reba Gonzales, Rebecca and Richard's infant daughter, shows signs of cowgirlism already. When she cries, her parents don't use a pacifier; instead they sit her on her horse's back and the sobs dissolve instantly into a broad, toothless smile.

Whether the children dream cowgirl and cowboy dreams or not, ranch families seem close-knit. When Cindy Price goes out to mend a fence, her three-year-old either tags along behind her asking questions or naps in the back of the Suburban while mom works. Kim Barmann, a New Mexico cowgirl, takes her two young daughters along most days when she pushes cows. Mother and children pile onto an all-terrain vehicle and talk as they ride, discussing cattle, day school, and Ninja Turtles.

Most ranches function as family coops, where everybody pulls his or her own weight, and kids routinely make decisions affecting the entire family's financial picture. In school, cowkids learn how to read and write and solve algebra problems. At home they're taught the proper way to rope a steer, deliver a calf, and strike a business deal. Wyoming cowgirl Tracy Risinger remembers pulling shifts as a midwife during calving season when she was a teenager. She'd sleep in her clothes in the middle of winter and set her alarm to ring every few hours so she could go out to the barn and check on the mothers-to-be. "Most of the time I could handle a delivery alone, but the main thing you learn growing up on a ranch is when to ask for help."

In the ladies' room at Denim & Diamonds in Santa Monica, cowgirls in poured-on slacks remousse their hair. Outside, near the dance floor, men and women who've never been near a rodeo chute tip their hats and shuffle their boots and grip longneck bottles of beer. Not all the revelers have had time to slip into their Bonanza wear; some of the men stand out in neckties and pinstripes, and a few of the women sport nine-to-five wardrobes as well. This is the modern barn dance, a genuine cosmopolitan postmodern hootenanny. Here, and at other such urban hoedown hangouts, twangy country songs alternate with rap and rock 'n' roll, creating a sort of Gene-Autry-meets-Hammer kind of mix. Everybody can be a cowboy or a cowgirl for a little while—at least until closing time.

In a city full of trendy pickup spots, why frequent a nouveau honky-tonk? For one thing the touch dancing featured at country-and-western clubs makes it easier to strike up conversations. The girls working with the mousse say they come for the cowboys. Sure, most of these guys wouldn't know which end of a branding iron to heat, but they act like cowboys. They have nice manners and make

pleasant conversation and like to have a good time. "You know, like Garth Brooks or Clint Black or something," the women say.

In the men's room, the cowboys probably take similar pains combing their mustaches and adjusting their Stetsons to the perfect "howdy there, honey" angle. If the moussers in the ladies' room see Denim & Diamonds as a smorgasbord of cowboy flesh, a ranch-style disco with wall-to-wall Marlboro men, the mustache groomers lingering at the urinal see it as a place to meet "girls who look like that woman in the Guess jeans ad."

Big-city cowboy Hunter Nelson hopes to find his Ms. Right Cowgirl at The Rose, a swanky country-and-western nightclub in Houston. He comes in most Thursdays, has a few beers, dances a little, and sometimes meets a woman he'll see again. If Hunter ran a personal ad to find his very own Dale Evans, it would read: *Fun-loving cowboy seeks bodacious, long-legged thoroughbred filly with enough personality to start a stampede. Education a plus. Sense of humor a must* . . . Ah, if only Hunter had lived a hundred years ago, he could have made Miss Ellen Callahan one happy cowgirl.

CHAPTER FIVE

SWEETHEARTS OF THE RODEO

THEY CALL Charmayne James Rodman the "Million-Dollar Cowgirl." When she rides into town, people sit up and take notice. Her entourage, human and horseflesh, plows a wide row. The vehicles in her caravan—a deluxe Dodge pickup truck she earned in competition and a customized horse trailer–dressing room— are color-coordinated. Even though her performing clothes hang in a special closet in the traveling barn, bellhops lug half a dozen pieces of luggage up to her suite. Like a western-style Madonna or Elizabeth Taylor, the Million-Dollar Cowgirl draws attention in a crowd. Part athlete, part entertainer, she has amassed a mini-fortune by piloting her famous horse, Scamper, around three barrels in less time than it takes most gals to pull their boots on. Consecutive eight-time world-champion barrel racer Charmayne James Rodman reigns supreme as the current sweetheart of the rodeo.

Now in her early twenties, Charmayne picked up her first championship belt buckle at age fourteen. She kept up with her homework by mail, and took her final high school graduation tests between runs at a rodeo in 1990. From her home in Galt, California, she drives from state to state for rodeos with her husband, team roper Walt Rodman. Between barrel runs, Charmayne fills out deposit slips. During the past eight years, Charmayne's total winnings have rolled into the seven digits, making her rodeo's first Million-Dollar Cowgirl.

Cowgirls aren't the only women who say "Hey, look at me" by con-

fronting big animals in tight spaces. Lady jockeys do it every day. Female polo players swing mallets alongside male teammates. Women fight bulls in Spain and Mexico. And Marilyn Quayle, wife of the former Vice President, is one of several notable women showing off in cutting-horse competitions from time to time.

But nothing serves as a better forum for western showmanship than the rodeo. Spanish speakers pronounce it "ro-DAY-oh" like Los Angeles's swank Rodeo Drive. Real American cowgirls drawl "RO-dee-oh." Country music star Reba McEntire, a frequent rodeo entertainer, once summed it up this way: "RO-dee-oh is where you make money, and ro-DAY-oh is where you spend it."

Today rodeo competitions are broadcast by ESPN. *Sports Illustrated* occasionally publishes profiles of rodeo stars. At some southwestern colleges and universities, rodeo ranks as a varsity sport where a student athlete might letter in, say, bull riding. But is it really sport? Or is it show business? Highly skilled clowns, deflecting agitated livestock away from thrown riders, play a part in the rodeo spectacle. And the grand entry—an elaborate horseback parade of celebrities, beauty queens, and local politicos—opens the show. Most rodeo cowgirls wear eye-catching outfits and stage makeup into competition. In this light, rodeo looks more like a Las Vegas extravaganza than an athletic tournament. The honchos at the Professional Rodeo Cowboys Association describe rodeo simply as a "uniquely American phenomenon."

The phenomenon has supplied America with some unique heroines. Give a gal a rope, a horse, a small enclosure, and out of the chute charges a folk goddess able to perform fabulous feats anytime, anywhere.

The earliest rodeos resembled Wild West shows, but featured extended cowboy contests. Cowpokes, a group with an unusual propensity for creating verbs from nouns, referred to performing in the shows as "wild westing."

Sometimes called "stampedes," "roundups," or "pioneer day celebrations" these prototypical rodeos often kicked up dust on Independence Day, a holiday known in some parts as "the cowboy's

LET'S RODEO

All Roundups Are Not Created Equal

- **The National Finals Rodeo**. Las Vegas, NV. Mid-December. The best of the best.
- **The All-Girl Rodeo**. Hereford, TX. Mid-August. Cowgirls stay on longer.
- **The Calgary Stampede**. Calgary, Alberta. First week in July. Cowboy fun Canadian style.
- **The Texas Gay Rodeo**. In a different Texas city each year. Mid-November. Gay and lesbian rodeo hands whoop it up and buck convention.
- **Cheyenne Frontier Days**. Cheyenne, WY. Mid-July. "The Daddy of Them All."
- **The Prison Rodeo**. Huntsville, TX. Every Sunday in October. Cowboys wearing black-and-white stripes have nothing left to lose.
- **National Little Britches Finals Rodeo**. Colorado Springs, CO. Mid-August. The littlest cowboys and cowgirls.
- **Senior Pro Rodeo Finals**. Reno, NV. Mid-November. Geriatric buckaroos still in the saddle.
- **The George Strait Roping**. Kingsville, TX. Mid-May. Roping only.
- **Prescott Frontier Days**. Prescott, AZ. Early July. The oldest continuous rodeo in America.
- **Houston Livestock Show & Rodeo**. Houston, TX. Late February, early March. The biggest of big rodeos.
- **Bullnanza** (formerly Bullmania). Guthrie, OK. Early February. Man *vs.* bull.
- **La Fiesta de Los Vaqueros**. Tucson, AZ. Late February. Ro-DAY-oh with a Spanish accent.
- **West of the Pecos Rodeo**. Pecos, TX. Early July. The first organized rodeo in America.
- **California Rodeo**. Salinas, CA. Late July. Kicking up dust since 1911.

Christmas." The July Fourth festivities in many a ramshackle town included relay races, bronc-riding, and steer-roping contests, along with a few Wild West show elements, such as a reenactment of a stagecoach robbery or a make-believe pony express ride. Prescott, Arizona's rodeo started in 1888 and remains a yearly event—the oldest annual rodeo in the country. Cheyenne's Frontier Days started in 1897. The National Western Stock Show and Rodeo in Denver began in 1906, the California Rodeo at Salinas in 1911.

The heroics at these first rodeos were performed exclusively by men. But since no rules prohibited them from doing so, women soon saddled up for rodeo roughhousing, too, asking rhetorically, "Where's it written that we can't?" Annie Shaffer of Arkansas rode a bucking horse at a rodeo in 1896. The next year Bertha Blancett straddled a bronc and raced wild horses at Cheyenne's Frontier Days.

A few years later when Prairie Rose Henderson tried to sign up for the broncobusting competition at Cheyenne, the judges attempted to turn her away, saying, "No women allowed." Prairie Rose showed her thorns, demanding to see the rules. Since no clause specifically prohibited women from riding, she entered and competed, but didn't win. (In later rodeos Prairie Rose fared better, capturing many cowgirl titles. But her most perilous ride of all wasn't in an arena; it came when she and her horse trotted out into a Wyoming blizzard one night, never to return. Prairie Rose's body was finally recovered years later, identifiable only by the championship belt buckle she'd earned in rodeo competition.)

As early as the 1930s, Americans hailed rodeo a national institution. And while most early-day rodeoers had obtained their skills in the practical way, through ranch work, some non-cowboy types flocked to the 101 Ranch in Ponca City, Oklahoma, for a crash course in how to be a rodeo star—sort of an Introduction to Cowboying 101. A professional rodeo circuit developed. Competitive cowboys and cowgirls "hauled" from town to town to try for the steadily increasing prize money being dangled for the most spectacular rides. Some cowhands found rodeo a more lucrative business than ranching. At eight seconds a ride, the hours couldn't be beat.

Cowboys and cowgirls joke: "All it takes to be a good bronc rider is a weak head and a strong back." Funnily enough, the folks who say this are often wearing championship belt buckles. Whether they challenge wild horses, ride bulls, wrestle steers, or race barrels, rodeo hands were dealt courage in spades. Rodeo pits the "cowboy that can't be throwed" against the "horse that can't be rode," and fans have long loved witnessing the outcome of the matchup.

For most people the mention of rodeo brings to mind images of

HEAD GAL!

NANCY IS PRESIDENT OF THE GIRL'S RODEO ASSOCIATION WHICH DRAWS YOUNG RIDERS FROM FAR AND WIDE TO RISK THEIR NECKS.

THEY MAY NEED A NEW PREXY TOMORROW!

Nancy **BINFORD**

(WILDORADO, TEX.) THE GIRLS HELD THEIR BIG SHOW AT CHILDRESS, TEX RECENTLY

NANCY IS NOT ONLY PRESIDENT SHE TAKES AN ACTIVE PART AND COMPETES IN THE TOUGHEST EVENT— RIDING **BULLS!**

-1950

broncobusting—a cowboy flopping rag-doll style on the back of an angry horse, his free hand thrashing the air like a windshield wiper gone wild. Bronc riding figured prominently in early rodeo and remains popular today in two forms: bareback and saddle bronc riding. The events are similar. The bareback rider hangs on with one hand to a handle attached to a "rigging" cinched around the horse's middle. The saddle bronc rider uses a special saddle, grasping with one hand a rein attached to the animal's halter. Both saddle and bareback bronc riders mount the horse in a chute. When the cowboy gives the ready signal, the chute's gate flies open, and the horse blasts into the arena. A bronc rider must stick to the horse's back for eight seconds to score, while judges evaluate both his and the bronc's performance. The horse is rated on the ferociousness of his attempts to dethrone the rider; the rider gets points for his ability to stay aboard. If it sounds simple, it's not. Rodeo hands compare it to riding a jackhammer one-handed, except not that easy. All sorts of technicalities—how the cowboy spurs, how far back in the saddle he leans, how high he lifts his knees, how he holds his free hand—figure into the final assessment of a ride.

When women began bronc riding in the late 1800s, a few minor procedural allowances were made for them. Cowgirls usually rode gentler horses, animals selected by stock suppliers to "show pretty and buck high" for a dramatic-looking but somewhat safer ride. Some women competed "hobbled" with a piece of leather tied under the horse's belly from one stirrup to the other, making it impossible for the cowgirl to spur but easier for her to stay in the saddle. Hobbles were recommended, but not required, for trail-blazing rodeo cowgirls. The gals who rode "slick," without hobbles, earned extra points in competition along with reputations as real tough sisters.

THE COWGIRL POET

Relapse

By Audrey Hankins

AA books and Coors cans—
Fresh starts, forgotten vows.
Everything of yours
Wears the "hard-use" brand
Earmarked by neglect.

Through prisms of tears
Somber shadows and fears
I watch you mount
That same old bronc
And know he'll kill you yet.

The unexpected came to be expected when a cowgirl climbed aboard the hurricane deck of a pitching horse. Tad Lucas, the late legend from Fort Worth, was reportedly rodeoing to the tune of $12.000 per year by 1935. Once Tad drew a bronco so menacing that her husband Buck made a point of being nearby when she emerged from the chute. Sure enough, Buck had good reason to worry. The wild animal shook Tad from the saddle quickly. She went flying through the air, landing smack dab in Buck's waiting arms.

Tad had no trouble dismounting that particular day. But because of the hobbles, cowgirls often relied on the mounted pickup

ROPING WITH THE ONE YOU LOVE

Husband-Wife Team Roping: The Mixed Doubles for the Cattle Set

Two horses, two riders, one confused steer. Team-roping attempts to create order from chaos. "It's like trying to paint your fingernails in the middle of a dust storm," one roper says. Another calls it "the ballroom dancing of the rodeo world."

Here's how the choreography works: One team member is the "header" in charge of lassoing the steer's head; the other is the "heeler" responsible for securing the animal's hind hooves. At the start, the steer stands in a chute—the header on his horse behind an adjacent barrier on the left, the heeler on the right. When the buzzer sounds, the steer blasts into the arena, followed a few seconds later by the header, and a few seconds more by the heeler. The header ropes first, catching the horns or neck, then dallying his rope around the saddle horn and riding to the left to turn the steer away from the heeler. As header rides away, the heeler ropes the steer's hind feet. The clock stops when both ropes go taut with the riders facing each other.

For many ranch families, team roping has become a couples hobby, like playing dominoes or golf or tennis. One cowgirl maintains that the sport saved her marriage: "It was better than therapy because it taught us how to work together to solve problems." In Arizona, a team-roping cowgirl and her partner husband sometimes invite other couples over on Sundays for barbecue and little casual roping. "Yeah, sometimes we switch partners," she jokes, "husband swapping."

Couples get hooked on the sport. One woman continued heeling in weekend jackpot competitions through her sixth month of pregnancy. A neighbor asked this gal what her doctor thought about her roping while in a motherly way. "He thinks I'm a pretty good heeler," the cowgirl replied truthfully.

GREENER PASTURES

A Horse Obituary from Women's Pro Rodeo News

On October 16 Joyce Loomis's wonderful horse Dude died at the ripe old age of twenty-eight. He was spending his last days belly-high in grass by the side of Loomis's home in a pen where Joyce could view him. His companions were Bobbie Jo's first pony and Monika, the mare that carried Bob to many reining wins in the early seventies.

War Leo Dude, foaled in 1963, was bought in May of 1968 in Nebraska because of Kathie O'Brien's horse Jude who was such a good one. Dude was full brother to O'Brien's Warrior Leo—both by War Leo. Their mother was the dam of eight barrel horses.

Dude made the 1969 National Finals with just twenty rodeos. In 1970 he started out by winning the first four rodeos of the year. He led the entire year and finished by winning the finals—sharing runs with Donna Patterson's gelding Engle loaned to Joyce for the NFR. Dude set a new money-winning record at that time—the first to break $10,000 by winning $10, 600.

He was very consistent and a delight to haul. People would come and get Joyce thinking Dude was dead or sick. Dude would lie down and rest anywhere, any time, and ate the same way.

Dude won for every owner that had him after Loomis. He had forty-nine American Quarter Horse Association points in barrel racing and several youth points.

Dude and Joyce won the Astrodome American Quarter Horse Association Show twice.

Bob Loomis bought Dude back for Joyce to retire about seven years ago. Dude did not have a rider on his back after that.

men to free them from the saddle after a rough ride. Oldtimers in rodeo circles tell of a buxom broncobusting cowgirl whose blouse got hung up on the saddle horn. When the horse pitched, her shirt and underclothes were torn off, leaving her nude from the waist up, her considerable bosom heaving up and down each time the bronc leapt skyward. The gallant pickup cowboy dashed to the cowgirl Godiva's rescue. As she was plucked from the saddle, nearly naked, the woman reputedly said: "Get me off this horse before I black both my eyes."

Untamed horses provided plenty of excitement for riders and onlookers. But some early-day rodeo hands sought an even scarier thrill. They found it on the backs of angry, slobber-slinging bulls. Most rodeo events originated on the ranches and cattle drives of the Old West as natural extensions of stock work. But bull riding got started as just a crazy cowboy dare. For this event, a flat-braided length of manila rope is wrapped around the animal just behind the shoulders. Wearing a special glove coated with sticky resin, the cowboy fastens one hand under this rope rigging. When the bull charges out of the chute the cowboy must stay astride for eight seconds without "clawing leather" or allowing his free hand to touch himself or his reluctant mount. Spurring to make the bull buck more fiercely is not mandatory, but a cowboy usually earns extra points for it. As in bronc riding, the cowboy gets a score for his ride, and the bull pulls points for his degree of unpleasantness.

Rodeo cowgirl Vera McGinnis rode bulls often in the years before World War I. She described her first bullish encounter this way: "The animal was so wide I felt as if I were straddling the dining-room table, and to top everything else, his hide was loose, and I rolled around like butter on a hot plate. It reminded me of hopscotch. Two feet here and two feet there, hitting the ground with almost a ton of belligerence at every bounce."

Vera and other gutsy gals usually made out just fine seated atop cantankerous rodeo bulls. But taking steers down for the count—well, that could be a bit trickier. With a very few exceptions, bulldogging or steer wrestling is an all-male rodeo event, and always has been. In this event, a two-hundred-pound human goes hand to horn with a 750-pound steer. The cowboy flings himself from the back of a gal-

loping horse onto a running head of beef. The race is against the clock. Once the man has snagged the steer, he tries to throw it to the ground faster than the competition. It's easy to see why big cowboys, the linebackers of the rodeo world, have long been the elite of bull-dogging. And why cowgirls—heavy on courage and light on poundage—tend to shine more brightly in other rodeo events.

Lucille Mulhall and other ground-breaking cowgirls did carve out a niche in steer tying—a surprising fact considering how big the beef and how small the cowgirls. In standard steer tying, not to be confused with the similar game called calf roping, a mounted cowgirl or cowboy approaches a running steer and throws a loop around the animal's horns. Then, casting slack to the right side of the saddle horn, the competitor and his horse move left, jerking the steer off its feet. While the horse keeps the rope taut, the rider dismounts and uses a "pigging string" to tie the steer's legs with three fast loops and a "hooey," or hitch to secure the wrap.

Lucille regularly took trophies at turn-of-the-century steer-tying contests, in which she competed against men. Her strategy involved careful analysis of the competition, and a secret weapon—a shorter rope. Permitted during the unrestricted days of early rodeo, a few feet less rope between the cowgirl and the steer allowed her to ride closer to her quarry and then to make a harder trip.

Early rodeo women took a special shine to a few events and made them their own. Horse racing and trick riding seemed particularly suited to a feminine touch. Nothing like the Kentucky Derby, rodeo horse racing was run as a relay event in which women rode one horse one lap around an oval track, then changed to a second mount for a second loop, and then to a third for the final dash to the finish line. The excitement of the relays came when the cowgirls changed mounts. At some rodeos the jockeys stopped one horse, dismounted, and climbed aboard the next, sometimes taking their saddles with them. At other tracks, they pulled the first horse to a halt so that the animal's head rested precisely on the rump of the second horse; then, the riders "pony expressed" from saddle to saddle without touching the ground. Another relay method called "lettin' 'er fly" involved vaulting from one moving horse onto another.

RODEO UNIVERSITY

So You Want to Be a Cowgirl

They say the great ones are born, not made. But aspirants willing to plop down from $100 to $750 can enroll in Rodeo U and learn from the masters:

BARREL RACING

- **Kirby Rodeo School**. P.O. Box 266, Comanche, OK 73529. (405) 439-6358. Three-day barrel-racing clinics with 1978 World Champion Connie Kirby, plus occasional bull-riding lessons with her husband Butch Kirby, 1978 World Champ and current rodeo judge.
- **Sharon Camarillo Clinics**. P.O. Box 6433, Chico, CA 95927. (916) 895-1852. Many-time California State Barrel-Racing Champion Sharon Camarillo teaches two-day clinics all over the U.S., as well as in Canada and Australia.

CALF ROPING

- **Josey Enterprises Inc**. Route 2, Box 235. Karnack, TX 75661. (903) 935- 5358. Pick up the basics of calf roping and barrel racing at frequent two- and three-day clinics, or at the annual one-week seminar taught by four-time world-champion barrel racer Martha Josey.

ROUGH-STOCK RIDING/BULLFIGHTING

- **Jan Youren Rodeo School**. Garden Valley, ID 83622. (208) 462-3730. Three-day bareback- and/or bull-riding classes with rough-stock champ Jan Youren.
- **Sankey Rodeo Schools**. Route 1 Box 781, Branson, MO 65616. (417) 334-2513. Two- to four-day bull riding, bronc riding, saddle-bronc riding, and occasional bullfighting clinics conducted by Lyle Sankey, two-time national bull-riding title holder.

TEAM ROPING

- **Doyle Gellerman/Walt Woodard Roping School**. 4214 East Arch, Stockton, CA 95215. (209) 462-0973. More than fifty three-day clinics per year held in the U.S., Canada, and Australia by world-class roping team Doyle Gellerman and Walt Woodard.

STEER WRESTLING

- **Butch Myers Steer Wrestling School**. Route 6, Box 6455, Athens, TX 75751. (903) 675-1532. Three-day lessons led several times each year by Butch Myers, steer-wrestling pro and 1980 World Champ.

Relay races were sometimes accompanied by a heat or two of Roman racing, in which the jockeys stood upright, reining two horses simultaneously, with one foot planted on each animal's back. Roman racing as well as rodeo trick riding also eventually came to be largely dominated by women. For trick-riding events, each cowgirl submitted a list of stunts and then prepared to perform any trick from her repertoire upon demand. The stunts fell into three categories: "top work" for various stands in the saddle; "vaults," executed by touching the ground with the feet; and "drags," accomplished by grasping special straps on the tack then hanging off the side or back of the horse. Trick riders were rated on grace, skill, degree of difficulty, and speed of the horse among other considerations. Rodeo audiences just couldn't get enough.

For western girls of the 1910s and 1920s, signing on with a rodeo was akin to joining a circus or a Broadway chorus line. Some speculated that a rodeo championship might even pave an easy road to a silent-film career. Cowgirl Bertha Blancett was one who rode the rodeo to Hollywood. There, she found work as a stunt rider. Early on, the show-business aspect of rodeo required that pretty be a part of the cowgirl's presentation. The more delicate and feminine a competitor appeared to be, the more the audiences marveled at her portfolio of macho skills. By the time rodeo galloped into the modern era, glamour was already part of the cowgirl mystique.

The modern era of professional rodeo began just after World War II. Since then ladies' participation in mainstream competitions has been largely limited to grand entry parades, rodeo-queen beauty pageants, and barrel racing. Gals specializing in roping and rough-stock riding have been relegated to low-money jackpots or a few all-girl contests. Today, only six or so rodeos currently sponsor women's rough-stock competitions.

The change started during the Depression of the 1930s. Since both relay and Roman racing required multiple mounts for each rider, and since stock suppliers typically provided separate buckers for women's events, the costs of maintaining and transporting the animals needed for women's rodeo far exceeded the meager prize

LAS MATADORAS

Cowgirls de la Corrida

Two hundred years ago the Spanish artist Francisco Goya slipped a cartoonish depiction of a female matador into one of his works as a joke. Today, there's no laughter in the bull ring when a woman takes up the cape.

Juanita Cruz started it all. She challenged bulls in the plazas of Madrid and Seville before the Spanish Civil War. At first Juanita hid behind the name Señorita X so her family would not discover the heresy she committed by trespassing into the macho world of bullfighting. Instead of the regular matador's *traje de luces* or suit of lights, Juanita wore skirts into the bull ring. She was fearless. Even when she dropped her cape, she never fled a charging *toro*.

"If I were a man, I would run," she once said. "But if I run, someone in the audience will yell that I am running because I am a woman and I am scared—so I will not run."

Juanita retired in 1947, and died in 1981. But a new generation of brave young women have taken up the cape. Christina Sánchez has been hailed as one of the most promising of a new breed of *matadoras*. Her bravery, aristocratic carriage, and fluid cape work earned her honors as the best *torero* in her class at the Tauromaquia de Madrid, an institute devoted to the art of bullfighting.

"I want to be a woman who changes men's thinking," she has said, "Bullfighting makes me feel big inside. Bullfighting is to dream awake . . . Every problem in your life goes away in front of a bull. Because this problem, the bull, is bigger than all other problems."

Christina masters her bullish opponents on foot. Marie Sara Bourseiller conquers them *rejoneador* style—or from horseback with a barbed lance. Fans call Mexican *rejoneadora* Karla Sánchez "La Princesa Rubia" or the blond princess. She battles bulls from horseback too. As the famous matador Antonio Ordóñez once said when discussing the girls garnering glory in his field, "If women are capable of fighting four-year-old bulls, what are men going to do to stand out from them? All that will remain for us is to give birth."

Spanish matadora Christina Sanchez.

money offered. With the outbreak of World War II, all-girl rodeos briefly came into vogue. While cowboys battled Axis powers overseas, cowgirls kept the rodeo fires burning at home. But like the All-American Girls Professional Baseball League—an enterprise begun by big-league executives should war cause a scarcity of male players—the all-girl rodeo craze was short-lived. Today the women-only rodeo circuit continues, but on a much smaller scale.

Most major present-day pro rodeos are held under the auspices of the Professional Rodeo Cowboys Association. They generally offer saddle-bronc riding, bareback riding, bull riding, calf roping, and steer-wrestling contests for men, and barrel racing only for women.

In barrel racing, a cowgirl and her horse charge across a starting line and run a cloverleaf pattern around three barrels, racing the clock. Timing begins when the horse's nose reaches the starting line. It stops when his nose crosses the finish. The cowgirl approaches barrel one, passes a hair to the left of it and makes a complete turn. Then she gallops to barrel two, passes to the right and makes a complete turn. At barrel three, she also zooms right, turns, and then hauls to the finish line. Or, if she prefers, the cowgirl can run the pattern in the opposite direction. Knocking over one of the fifty-five-gallon steel barrels draws a five-second penalty. There's no world record, because the distance between barrels differs in each arena.

The 2,000-member Women's Professional Rodeo Association governs barrel racing, and the 125-member Professional Women's Rodeo Association oversees roping and rough-stock riding events at a handful of all-girl rodeos each year.

Somewhat as in the Olympics, each event at a rodeo produces a single winner. Cowboys often compete in more than one event, so the fellow who racks up the highest cumulative score wins the Best All-Around Cowboy title. At rodeos where women compete in more than one event, an All-Around Cowgirl trophy goes out too. Prize money ranges from $25 in small local jackpot roping events to $2.5 million at the National Finals Rodeo in Las Vegas. The booty isn't just money either. Belt buckles, ornate saddles, fancy spittoons and sometimes even new pickup trucks go to the winners at mega rodeos. The Professional Rodeo Cowboys Association sanctions about 800 rodeos

THE MINORS' LEAGUE

Little Britches Rodeo

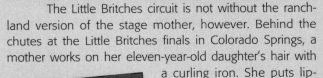

Rodeo gets in the blood early. Ranch kids ride before they walk. They rope by preschool, run barrels in kindergarten, and start rodeoing by second grade.

The National Little Britches Rodeo Association sanctions more than a hundred juvenile events each year for children aged eight to eighteen. Kiddie cowgirls and cowboys win trophies and ribbons instead of cash, and at the annual finals, winners take home college scholarships.

Ten-year-old Kashley Hughes of Model, Colorado, has won two All-Around Little Britches Cowgirl championships. She'd rather rope than join the Campfire Girls, or practice barrel racing than ride her bike.

Blandi Sargent, age ten, takes rodeo less seriously. She's been racing barrels since she was five, but these days she's just as enthusiastic about soccer and softball as competitive rodeo. Blandi's parents think that's fine. "As long as she enjoys it, I enjoy it," her mom says. "When she gets more into cheerleading or something else, that'll be fine, too."

The Little Britches circuit is not without the ranchland version of the stage mother, however. Behind the chutes at the Little Britches finals in Colorado Springs, a mother works on her eleven-year-old daughter's hair with a curling iron. She puts lipstick on the child, and reminds her to "smile, smile, smile." By the time the announcer calls the little girl's number, her face has been painted up like a pre-teen floozy. The buzzer screams and the glamour girl gallops into the arena and promptly wrestles down a goat. When she looks up, accepting the crowd's applause, her face is covered with mud, and her hair is a rat's nest of hairspray and fallen curls, but she's smiling, smiling, smiling. The mother might see rodeo as a road her child can take to stardom, the child seems to see it as good time and a fun way to get dirty.

ENOUGH ROPE

"THE WEDDING BAND" MADE ALMOST EASY

Make a big loop in an eighteen-foot rope. Hold rope end in your right hand. Allow the honda to hang three feet below. You will have a full-sized loop to hold with your first and second finger.

Grass honda

With your left hand grasp the loop part of the rope. Extend rope in your right hand above your head. Move your left hand to your left never raising it any higher than your waist.

Hold your left hand steady. Raise your right hand to arm's length. Bring arm forward toward your head. Lower arm to your waist. Drop the loop while moving your right hand in a circular motion to the left. Continue spinning the rope. Yee Haw!!

annually. It's not unusual for male and female professionals on the circuit to throw their hats into the ring a hundred or so times each year.

Competitors say that rodeo grabs them by the guts and doesn't let go. The bug bites fans too. Each February when the rodeo descends on Houston, the entire city catches the fever. During the two-week run of the Houston Livestock Show and Rodeo, more than 1.5 million people crowd the Astrodome to witness the sport's top cowhands ride for a half-million-dollar purse. Between the steer wrestling and barrel racing, big-name country-music stars entertain each evening. The rodeo midway—with freak shows, Ferris wheels, and a photo concession selling snapshots that create the illusion of bull riding—stays open until midnight. During rodeo time, pinstriped Houston bankers wear fringed Daniel Boone jackets to work in downtown office towers. Television anchorwomen "go Texan" and read the news sporting bolo ties and cactus-shaped earrings. The mayor and the city council saddle up to lead the rodeo parade. And on the Friday before the rodeo begins, six thousand trail riders trot into town on horseback, clogging freeways and creating a surreal traffic jam—covered wagons on the interstate just a few miles from Mission Control.

In Fort Worth, the public schools close for one day so students can attend the Southwestern Exposition and Livestock Show. Tickets to the National Finals Rodeo in Las Vegas are as coveted as a pair of Wayne Newton passes. At the annual Lions' Club Rodeo in tiny Jasper, Texas, a sedan with a bumper sticker I'M A RODEO-A-HOLIC doesn't belong to a competitor but to a local attorney. In the stands, another rodeo-goer wears a T-shirt: I'D RATHER BE BARREL RACING.

Everybody seems to love rodeo except animal-rights activists. For decades the Society for the Prevention of Cruelty to Animals has insisted that some aspects of rodeo amount to institutionalized torture of livestock. Vera McGinnis remembered a rodeo performance's being picketed in Europe by animal lovers during the 1920s. Even in Lucille Mulhall's day, advocates of animal rights argued that when a bull fell from a stage into an orchestra pit, it hurt the bull. Literature published by the Professional Rodeo Cowboys Association maintains

that the sport doesn't damage its four-legged participants. Rodeo, they say, "values its animals and staunchly protects them with rules specifically designed to prevent cruelty or inhumane treatment."

Rodeo women come in all ages, shapes, and sizes. Texan Fallon Taylor ranks as the youngest full-time barrel racer on the big-league circuit. She was born in 1982. Alma Evetts of California is the oldest. Now in her seventies, she was racing barrels before many of her current counterparts could gurgle "giddy up" to a rocking horse. Charmayne James Rodman is probably the richest. And teenager Angie Meadors might be the most glamorous.

Angie skips school to rodeo. Well, she doesn't exactly play hooky. Angie has permission from her parents to haul her horse from venue to venue and race barrels for big money. Somehow, she manages to squeeze in her high school studies between runs. Tall, slender, blond, Angie looks more like a fashion model than a ranch hand. She is a fashion model, as a matter of fact. She poses for Wrangler jeans advertisements and was snapped for an article in *Seventeen* magazine, too. Preparing her horse for competition, Angie wears pink lipstick and thick mascara; rhinestone earrings dangle from beneath her cowboy hat.

Angie's colleague Vana Beissinger headquarters in Florida. Like Angie, she also consistently ranks among the top ten money winners on the circuit. In 1990 Vana deposited more than $45,000 in rodeo earnings into her account. Those numbers don't reflect pure profit, however. Subtract from the total the cost of diesel for the pickup, entry fees, and travel expenses. Then figure in insurance for the cowgirl, her horse, and her truck and trailer. Add to all this the high emotional cost of living on the highway, and it's clear that most barrel racers run for a reason other than money. Vana does it because it's fun.

She hauls with her mom. Together they put about 60,000 miles per year on their one-ton King Cab pickup truck. Nine months out of twelve they live in the travel trailer they haul from rodeo to rodeo. Their dog tags along to keep things feeling homey, and Lotto Jet—the equine half of the Beissinger barrel-racing team—rides in style in his own portable barn.

Vana and most of her colleagues agree: a good horse is sixty to eighty percent of the successful barrel-racing equation. When Lotto Jet gets too old to compete, Vana plans to throw in the saddle blanket and go back home to Florida to study animal psychology. "Shoot, I drove all night last night from Florida to Texas. Today I'll ride for twenty seconds, put my horse away, and drive to New Mexico. When weekenders pick up $50, they're tickled. If I don't win something this week or next, I'm in trouble." Vana must make at least $30,000 this year, or she'll go in the hole.

Barrel racers usually park their trailers near the arena where they're working. If they stay in one town long enough, the girls sometimes organize a softball game. Other evenings they visit from trailer to trailer, gossiping mostly about horses—whose looks good, whose

seems tired. Vana celebrated her birthday last year in Denver with five other barrel racers and some bull riders. In April she and another barrel racer went to a movie, and in Fort Worth last summer she spent a full Saturday at the mall.

Life for the barrel racer means mostly driving: driving the truck down the interstate from rodeo to rodeo, and driving the horse from barrel to barrel. But not counting all the road time, the hours spent grooming and caring for the horse, and the practice time put in during the months at home, the barrel racer works about three minutes a week, roughly seventeen seconds per competitive run or "go" as the cowgirls say. When you think about it, on a pure hourly basis, world champion Charmayne James Rodman nets more per minute than almost any female professional in any field.

For Charmayne, Vana, Angie, and the few others able to step up and yank the udder of the barrel-racing cash cow, the rodeo circuit affords a good living. But if a woman wants to ride rough stock or rope steers, she'd better have another way to pay her bills.

Ronda Harrison, a top money winner in all-girl competition, doesn't make enough from rodeo to quit her day job teaching sixth grade in Oklahoma. Ronda understands why her male counterparts compete for more money—"there are more of them, and they've been at it longer"—but that doesn't mean she likes it. She's a little more puzzled by the lopsided dividends in the different divisions of women's rodeo—the barrel racers make much more than the all-around cowgirls. There are simply more barrel racers out there than ropers and rough-stock riders, she reckons. Until more women join the rodeo ranks, the all-around cowgirl crowd will have to maintain nine-to-fives.

A single mom, Ronda rodeos mostly in the summer, and takes her daughter Samantha along. So far Ronda has roped her way to high school and college titles and captured the All-Around Championship in Professional Women's Rodeo Association competition three times. She doesn't mess with bulls or broncs. "I don't ride rough stock. At least not on purpose," she says, laughing. "Sometimes I get on a wild horse at home, but not in the arena." Tie-down and breakaway calf roping, team roping, and occasionally goat tying and barrel racing are Ronda's events. "You're not risking your life roping," she says, "fingers maybe, but not your life."

Rough-stock riders risk more than fingers. Two-time world-champion bull rider Lynn "Jonnie" Jonckowski of Montana got stomped for the first time at rodeo school. It took 160 stitches and

lots of plastic surgery to repair her face, but she finished second in her bull-riding class—the only woman among 105 men. After the accident, Jonnie figured she'd be so ugly that there would be nothing else she could do for a living. But her injuries healed and today she believes she looks better than before. On another ride, she broke her arm in twelve places. And every one of her ribs has been cracked at least once. When Jonnie goes in for her regular physical checkup, she considers herself healthy if the doctor says, "I see no new fractures." She says, "It's pretty bad when you're on a first-name basis with your anesthesiologist."

Jonnie insists the broken bones seem mild when compared to the severe muscle tears and deep sprains incurred during a bum outing on a bull. "Sometimes the pain is so bad you throw up." Still, Jonnie keeps dusting herself off and limping right back to the chute, ready to swallow whatever meanness the next bull dishes out. Her bravery and tenacity have earned her quite a following. Members of the Nitty Gritty Dirt Band composed a song, "The Bullrider Is a Lady," about their friend Jonnie Jonckowski. A Hollywood production company has purchased the rights to base a movie on her life story.

Although a cowgirl through and through, Jonnie sees herself as more Lycra than leather. She says being in tiptop physical condition plays an important role in a ride, but that the true trick involves selective memory—"Try not to think about getting stomped, but about all the good rides you've had before."

Cowgirls like Jonnie Jonckowski seem ambivalent about pain. Maybe they have something to prove, to themselves or to society. Or perhaps the thrill of victory more than offsets the agony of defeat. Lady bull riders say their sport gives them a high they can't get from booze or drugs. Weak heads, strong backs, and a love of danger keeps them coming back for more. "When the sun is on your face," explains Jonnie, "why walk into the shade?"

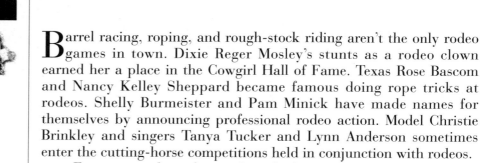

Barrel racing, roping, and rough-stock riding aren't the only rodeo games in town. Dixie Reger Mosley's stunts as a rodeo clown earned her a place in the Cowgirl Hall of Fame. Texas Rose Bascom and Nancy Kelley Sheppard became famous doing rope tricks at rodeos. Shelly Burmeister and Pam Minick have made names for themselves by announcing professional rodeo action. Model Christie Brinkley and singers Tanya Tucker and Lynn Anderson sometimes enter the cutting-horse competitions held in conjunction with rodeos.

For women, the rodeo road can be bumpy at times. Fern Sawyer encountered quite a pothole in 1934. When studying home economics at Texas Tech University, she was summoned by the dean of women one day. All dressed up, sitting nervously in the administrator's office, mischievous Fern just assumed she'd been caught doing something awful—she could only guess what. "I'd done plenty of things that could have gotten them upset," Fern remembers. Her crime on this particular day: she'd been seen participating in a rodeo.

"They were going to kick me out of school for rodeoing! Thought it was 'common' and all that," she recalls. "Now they have one of my suits in their museum, and they offer rodeo scholarships to women." Fern laughs when she tells the story; she appreciates the irony. The Million-Dollar Cowgirl appreciates it too. Thanks to women like Fern and Lucille Mulhall and Tad Lucas, Charmayne James Rodman can laugh all the way to the bank.

CHAPTER SIX

A GIRL AND HER COWS

REBECCA GONZALES doesn't put on any makeup before she goes to work. Sometimes she doesn't even brush her hair. She rolls out early, rubs the sleep from her eyes and gets right to business. No bagel. No aerobics. No morning newspaper.

The saddle is Rebecca's desk; the range her office. Her dress for success: Wrangler denims, dusty boots, jingling spurs. You can see by her outfit that Rebecca Gonzales is a cowgirl. And if the western garb doesn't spell it out clearly enough, the calluses on her hands and the fearless way she walks up behind a one-ton bull and slaps him playfully on the rump leave little doubt that this is no citified poser riding the latest fashion trend.

Rounding up a firm figure to represent exactly how many women in the United States share Rebecca's vocation can be tricky. The most recent Census of Agriculture gives the number as 46,000 plus change. But the actual cowgirl tally could go a lot higher or a lot lower than the government's data indicate. "I guess it all depends on who you call cowgirl," the census-office spokeswoman explains.

Well, let's see. Whom do we call cowgirl? We hear about rhinestone cowgirls and cosmic cowgirls and urban cowgirls and drugstore cowgirls and Coca-Cola cowgirls, and even cowgirls getting the blues. But unmodified and stripped down to its underwear, the term "cowgirl" refers

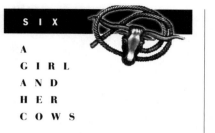

to a woman who makes her living raising cattle. A girl converting cows to cash.

Cows, horses, grass, rain, and land. Those elements define the real cowgirl's universe. Sure, nifty boots and silver buckles sometimes help a cow belle cut a more stylish silhouette in the saddle. And a well-furnished ranch house certainly adds a touch of refinement to evenings on the prairie. Handsome cowboys come with the territory. And every now and then in ranch country you might pass a big, "howdy-I'm-cattle" Cadillac—an obnoxious fire-engine red monstrosity with fins in back and steer horns wired to the front grill. At the wheel, there'll be that one-in-a-million showboatin' cattlewoman barreling down the interstate toward Dallas to celebrate the end of spring roundup. The true cowgirl, however, calls the campy Cadillac, cute cowboys, and adobe hacienda "gravy." Heifers, steers, and calves—these things she calls the staff of life.

Rebecca Gonzales's typical morning to-do list—moving cattle from one pasture to another, doctoring a sick calf, placing orders for feed, mending fences—may seem at first glance archaic. And in many ways it is. Even though the modern cattlewoman probably knows more about embryo transfers and genetics than she does about fancy roping or playing harmonica to soothe a restless herd, her primary concern remains the care and feeding of cows. But, if some snippets of Rebecca's workday conjure up images of scenes from an episode of *The Big Valley*, a few of her more scientific tasks sound almost Star Trek-like in their complexity. In the two centuries since ranching first took root in the southwestern United States, the process by which a rancher gets his or her stock from birth to barbecue grill has changed greatly—and at the same time not at all.

Why I Want To Be A Cow Girl
by Blaire Bresnan
Age 7½

I want to be a cow girl.
I Like the play guns. I
want to go to people's
House's and Shoot the play
gun in the air.   When I
was two I thought that
cow girls were girl cows!
I Like the outfit.

CHICKEN-FRIED GONADS

Bull Nuggets: The Mucho Macho Virility Snack

Battered and fried bovine testicles, mmmm good. In branch country they euphemistically call the tender delicacy "calf fries" or "Rocky Mountain oysters." But, hey, a gonad by any other name, right? This is no finger food for the faint of heart.

At roundup time, the young male calves not destined to become sires are liberated from their manhood and made steers. Cowpokes say it's painless. The animals are clamped in a "squeeze chute," and before they even know what happened a razor catches the sunlight, and they're mooing soprano. "There's some blood, and maybe a little discomfort," one cowgirl says, "but it's no big deal." Her husband doesn't really want to discuss it.

Once all the calves have been branded and vaccinated, dehorned and emasculated, it's chow time. First, the tough muscle that covers the testicle should be removed with a sharp knife. The bull nuggets should then be soaked in salty water for an hour or so to take off the blood. Next, parboil them for two or three minutes in water with a bit of vinegar and soda added. Rinse well. Dip them first in beaten egg, then in flour or bread crumbs seasoned with salt and pepper. Fry in hot lard until golden brown. Drain. Serve hot.

Cattle raising ranks alongside farming, mining, and fur trapping as one of the original North American business enterprises. And when you're talking North American firsts, you're talking Christopher Columbus. The Spanish cows he brought along on his second voyage in 1493 became the first to chew cuds in the New World. Descendants of the Columbus herd found contentment in Mexico (then called New Spain), and in 1540, when Francisco Vásquez de Coronado crossed the Rio Grande in search of treasure, five hundred head of fat and happy cattle accompanied the expedition as a sort of walking food supply.

In the two hundred years following Coronado's expedition, the Spanish established a handful of mission ranches, run by priests, in southern California. Padres also punched cows in what is today

Texas, the cradle of the American ranching industry. English-speaking colonists showed up in Texas in 1821. Since neither the conquerors nor the natives of New Spain had bothered to castrate their bulls or control the bovine population in any serious way, the Texas settlers found the open range crowded with cattle. In no time, Texans discovered they were onto something big with this beef and leather thing. A man who could sit a horse and swing a rope could pocket a profit without exposing any financial risk up front. Once the cow catchers had collected several hundred head along the Mexico border, they would drive them north to the greener plains of East Texas and sell them to the new colonists homesteading there. By 1840, some of the settlers had amassed nice-sized herds of cattle themselves, and they too started looking for bulk buyers. The first wave of cattle drives had begun.

During the two decades just after the Civil War, an estimated ten million Texas

BRAND NAMES

Why the Cow Wears Her Return Address

Cattle equaled currency in the fenceless days of the open range; and brands, the symbols burned into an animal's hide to denote ownership, served as a stockman's wallet—his safe.

Like a twenty-dollar bill on a city sidewalk, a stray longhorn didn't usually have time to get lonesome. Cowboys rounded up unbranded mavericks and welcomed them warmly into their own herds. Sometimes, cowboys were known to alter brands, thereby appropriating another fellow's beef. Using a piece of metal called a "running iron," a lowdown rustler might, for example, doctor a Double H to read as Double Box Arrow, and then trot the rechristened cow off to market as his own.

Today in cattle country, brands are registered in a ledger at the county clerk's office, and in some families the brand serves as more than a return address on livestock. It also creates a sort of prairie heraldry—the cowboy's coat of arms.

Running W

cattle strolled north with thirty-five thousand men prodding them forward. Open-range cowboys never mended fences. There were none. The grass and water and the land itself belonged to all.

At about the same time these vast rivers of legally and illegally tattooed longhorn cattle flowed out of Texas, the mighty herds of buffalo that had thrived on the great plains were being hunted to extinction. With the buffalo gone, the Native American civilizations were forcibly subdued, uprooted, and moved onto reservations. This cleared the way for farmers and cattlemen to appropriate the fertile flatland between the Mississippi River and the Rocky Mountains.

For a short time the entire middle of the country was like one big open pasture. But by the 1880s railroads, barbed wire, and the onslaught of settlers eager to take advantage of the land made available by the Homestead Act catapulted cattle ranching into a new era. Water and land now carried price tags. Cattlemen were forced to buy acreage and fence it. Unable simply to drive their herds somewhere else in winter, ranchers suddenly needed to devise ways to feed and water their stock. Although still the soul of the beef industry, cows ceased to be the primary tender in which stockmen dealt. Land held more lasting value. Cattle functioned like four-legged factories for making meat from grass, turning leafy green into folding green. The perspective changed. And ranching became an expensive and complicated way to make a living.

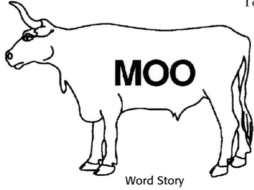

Broken Heart

Word Story

Today's beef grower is a generalist. An aspiring rancher attends a university to study animal science and agricultural economics. He reads *The Wall Street Journal* as well as the *The National Cattleman*. He pushes paper more than he prods cattle, and he might use a computer to

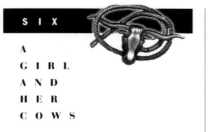

keep records on livestock and finances. Many of the largest ranches operate as corporations with boards of directors. These corporate cattle companies issue annual reports; their shares are traded on the stock exchange. And in this day of more-brains, less-brawn ranching, some of America's finest cattlemen are cattlewomen.

The ranch that Rebecca Gonzales and her husband Richard maintain on the Texas coast provides a snapshot of the American beef industry during the past few decades. The Gonzales's herd is one-fourth the size of the one Rebecca's father ran on the same land ten years ago, and at least a thousand animals fewer than her grandfather pastured here in the 1930s. Modern ranchers like Rebecca and Richard deal in more than hide and horn. The most profitable ranching operations these days are animal, vegetable, *and* mineral.

On *Dallas*, J.R. Ewing and his rich ranching buddies carried fat wallets and wore tuxedos with their Tony Lamas to the Cattle Baron's Ball. If you'll remember, J.R. had been graced with a little bit of oil on the side. It was that bubbling crude that kept young John Ross in

THE ROADKILL HALL OF FAME

A cowgirl coddles her cows, and can be downright fanatical in her devotion to her horse. But her heart hardens when certain other of God's creatures cross her path. Among the critters a cowgirl wouldn't mind meeting on the highway with the wheels of her pickup:

• Coyote	• Possum	• Mountain lion
• Armadillo	• Skunk	• Rattlesnake
• Deer	• Javelina	• Scorpion

good schools, and put food on the table at South Fork during the years when brucellosis, drought, or flat beef prices would likely have made cows more hobby than cash crop.

The oil-and-cattle partnership can't be dismissed as pure Hollywood fiction, however. Lots of cattlemen have been blessed with land buttered on both sides—nutrient-loaded grass growing on top and fossil fuel bubbling below. The "awl bidness," as they say in Texas. As one modern-day cowgirl jokes: "The best way to raise cattle is in the shade—the shade of an oil well." Rebecca Gonzales insists if a successful rancher talks truth about his financial picture, he's probably got a little oil money helping his livestock along. Her family's well blew in during the 1930s.

New Mexico cattlewoman Fern Sawyer is a colorful character well known in ranching, rodeo, political, and other circles. She remembers the day in 1949 when a wildcat well hit pay dirt on her family's property. "Daddy was just sick when he got that oil," she says laughing—sick because leaking pipelines typically mean curtains for cows and her father had spent his whole life developing strong breeds. Fern, on the other hand, was tickled by the petro-dollars. As soon as she wrapped her fingers around that first royalty check, Fern made tracks to Dallas, where she bought a Cadillac, a mink coat, and a diamond watch in a single afternoon. "My daddy said he might as well have thrown that money right back in the hole as to have given it to me 'cause I spent it all in one day." Of course, she didn't really fritter it all away in one day. Forty years after the first Sawyer well blew in, Fern still drives a big new Cadillac, and lives in one of the most tastefully decorated ranch houses anywhere.

Not all landowners hold cards as lucky as the Sawyers'. Generally speaking, ranching affords a good life but a poor living. The tennis courts and swimming pool of the legendary King Ranch illustrate the exception rather than the rule. The wealth of ranchers without the boon of oil deposits beneath their pastures is mostly on paper. Owners of spreads not speckled with pump jacks hauling up a few hundred barrels of crude each day must constantly prepare for the next market downturn. A popular rancher's parable tells of the fellow who asked a weathered-looking cowgirl what she'd do if she

suddenly struck oil and made millions. The cowgirl pondered this for a second and said, "Well, I reckon I'd just keep ranching until I used it all up."

In the 1980s, however, even oil stopped pumping dollars into ranch coffers. About the same time the easy money in the oil patch dried up, farm subsidies fell and many health-conscious Americans began eschewing red meat. All of this meant bad news for cow people. Drooping prices at the stockyard, along with the rising property values accompanying urban encroachment, prompted many ranchers to lease part of their acreage, trim their herds, and look for ways to supplement their ranching income.

The smart rancher's word for today: "diversification." Resourceful cattlewomen and cattlemen have dreamed up some pretty innovative ways of squeezing extra money out of their land. Many property owners lease acreage to hunters. More than one cattle outfit has been plucked from the brink of bankruptcy by rifle-bearing city dwellers willing to pay for the opportunity to bag a few superfluous white-tailed deer. Some hands pick up extra bucks in professional rodeos; others sell breeding stock on the side or do double duty as tour guides.

The Y.O. Ranch in Texas has diversified to such an extent that cattle sales today provide only a fraction of the operation's annual revenue. Tourism accounts for the rest. The savvy owners of the Y.O. have stocked their land with giraffes, zebras, and other exotic game, and offer safari-style hunts to visitors. They also manage first-class dude-ranching facilities, which for a time included a financial interest in the Y.O. Ranch Hilton Hotel. Even before the excitement generated by the movie *City Slickers*, Y.O. Ranch dudes had been opening their billfolds for the once-a-year chance to head 'em up and move 'em out as paid participants in an actual, for-real cattle drive and roundup. For those urbanites who just can't get enough of playing cowboy, one historic cattle company sells fifty to two-hundred-acre parcels of the ranch itself. Career cowhands snidely refer to these weekend ranching operations as "forty-forty programs" because they are undertaken by people who work forty hours a week and own just forty cows.

Rebecca and Richard Gonzales don't bunk dudes, but they have diversified. While ranching remains their primary gig, the couple lease a pure-bred Texas longhorn bull, Apache Brave, to the Wall Street firm of Merrill Lynch Pierce Fenner & Smith for use in television commercials. With a prime cow-calf pair bringing $850 to $1,000 on the current livestock market, Rebecca speculates that each couple of cows sold represents at least a few hundred hours of work. Ranching may be her first love, but at $250-plus per day, you might say Rebecca Gonzales is bullish on advertising.

Helen Campbell Kleberg of the King Ranch was said to have been the inspiration for the Elizabeth Taylor character in Giant.

The notion that Madison Avenue seems to Rebecca a more certain source of income than her prime Texas acreage says a mouthful about the precariousness of agribusiness. Cow folks jabber constantly of disasters most of us never noticed. For instance, a cowgirl recalling an event from the early 1970s says, "Yeah, I got married during the Crash of '73," and she's not talking about a stock-market downturn or an airplane wreck. Ask and she'll translate: A serious glut of cattle flooding the market created big headlines among beef growers in the year before Nixon resigned. Catastrophe on the scale of 1973 doesn't come along too often, but on a small ranch the wolf scratches constantly at the door. Financial ruin seems always right around the corner, and yet just another turn from there flickers a hint of miraculous redemption. The trick is in surviving from turn to turn.

Since the 1960s, the number of cattle ranches in the United States has shrunk by half. It makes you wonder: Are career ranchers slowly riding into the sunset?

Hardly. The cattle industry dips and soars, but never fades from sight. As breeders have responded to America's demand for leaner meat, the per capita consumption of beef shows signs of rebounding in the 1990s. The United States still leads the world in cattle production. Enrollment in acade-

PRAIRIE SKIRTS

Playing Cowgirl at the Estrogen Ranch

Remember Curly, the Jack Palance character in *City Slickers*? Well, Jane Koger plays that part in real life, except she's not nearly so tough-talking or scraggly-looking, and her dudes are always women.

On the Homestead Ranch in the Flint Hills of Kansas, Jane offers paying female guests a chance to play cowgirl. Through a program called "Prairie Women Adventures," gals of all ages can help deliver calves in February and March. Or they can schedule their vacations to coincide with castration time in May. Some sporty city slickers sign up for the Flint Hills rodeo in June. What pavement-dwelling nine-to-fiver wouldn't want to spend a sabbatical in the wide-open spaces? Preg-checking cows in the morning, inoculating calves in the afternoon—for some women the cowgirl fantasy beats a weekend at the beach.

Prairie Women, Box 2, Matfield Green, KS 66862 (316) 753-3465

mic programs such as Cornell University's various majors in agriculture and Texas Christian University's Ranch Management school, appears steady if not growing.

While many students at "cow colleges" are women, a degree in ag journalism or ag marketing isn't a prerequisite to punching cows. Wyoming cowgirl Tracy Risinger grew up participating in 4-H and other junior agricultural programs, but she pursued a degree in economics at college. Her thinking: "After a lifetime of cattle work I figured I'd mastered the basics of day-to-day ranching, and I knew I wouldn't be able to just casually pick up accounting, marketing, or psychology." So Tracy cowgirled her way through a small liberal-arts college by selling Simmentals. She studied history, literature, sociology in the classroom, and studied cows at home.

The road most women take to the ranch doesn't typically pass a major university. Even in this day, the more common trail for the career cowgirl begins at the altar or the funeral parlor: she either marries a cattleman or assumes ranch reins after a husband or father passes away. Legendary West Texan Hallie Stillwell, now in her nineties, married into the ranch life in 1918 and has felt right at home on the range ever since.

Hallie's life adventure began when covered wagons were still in use, and it continues in an age when helicopters are employed to round up cattle. Long before "diversification" became the cattlewoman's watchword, Hallie kept lots of irons in the fire. As a young single woman she taught in a small town on the Mexican border, where the threat of raids from Pancho Villa and his gang prompted her to keep a pistol handy in the one-room schoolhouse. Hallie's other sidelines have included stints as a beautician, justice of the peace, historian, and newspaper reporter. Sometimes, she's called upon to give lectures. Not long ago she spoke to a group of ranch women about how to overcome the isolation and loneliness of life far from town. Hallie's concise advice: "Keep busy."

Although Hallie mostly supervises ranch work from the comfort of a Jeep these days, she insists that cattle raising comes down to 1 percent glamour and 99 percent grit. When she arrived at her husband's Big Bend-area ranch house after their honeymoon, Hallie dis-

MEET BOSSY

A Primer for Non-Cowgirls

- **Family names**. Cattle belong to the genus *Bos*. Modern breeds come from two species: *Bos indicus*, the humped cattle of Asia, and *Bos taurus*, the wild cattle of Europe.
- **World citizens**. Cattle graze on every continent except Antarctica.
- **Rude, crude, lewd, rechewed food**. Cattle chew their food twice for proper digestion. They chew, swallow, then bring the food back up from the stomach and chew it some more. The vomit they chomp is called a *cud*.
- **That heifer looks like grandma**. In India, where Hindus believe the soul can be reincarnated in the body of different animals, cattle are deemed sacred.
- **Moo IQs**. Cattle are the slow learners of the barnyard. Not as intelligent as dogs or horses, cows don't usually respond when called by name.
- **Ma**. A *cow* is a female.
- **Pa**. A *bull* is a male.
- **John Boy**. A *steer* is a male without reproductive organs. A bovine eunuch.
- **Mary Ellen**. A *heifer* is a maiden cow. A debutante.

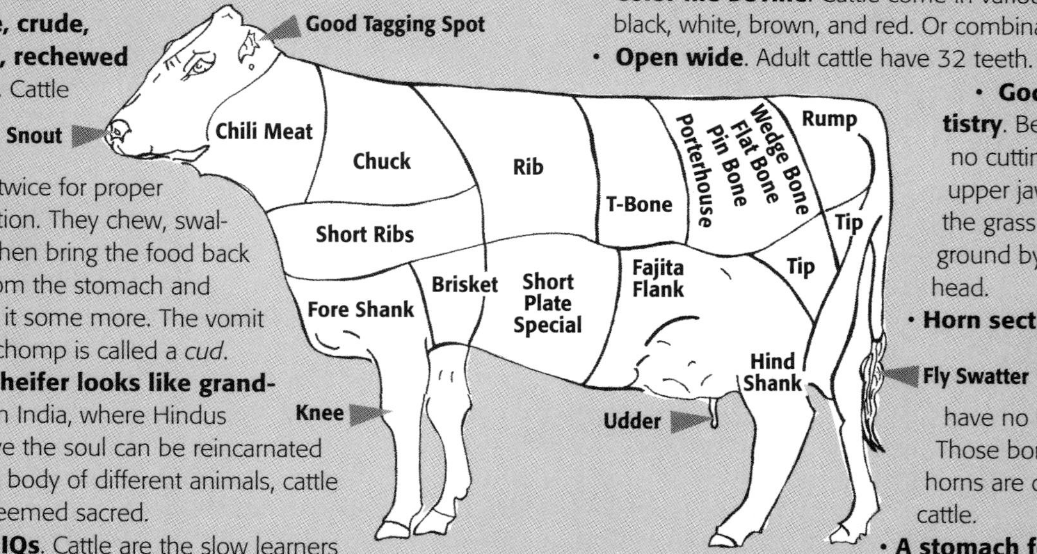

- **Jim Bob or Elizabeth?** A *calf* is a young heifer or bull.
- **Girlish figures**. Cows typically weigh 900 to 2,000 pounds.
- **Amazing hulks**. Bulls tip the scale at 2,000 pounds and up.
- **Color me bovine**. Cattle come in various shades of black, white, brown, and red. Or combinations thereof.
- **Open wide**. Adult cattle have 32 teeth.
- **God and dentistry**. Because it has no cutting teeth in its upper jaw, a cow tears the grass from the ground by moving its head.
- **Horn section**. Cattle horns are hollow and have no branches. Those born without horns are called *polled* cattle.
- **A stomach for every occasion**. Cattle are *ruminants*, and have stomachs with four compartments: *rumen*, *reticulum*, *omasum*, and *abomasum*.
- **Udder delight**. Beef cows produce milk only for their calves, and have smaller udders than dairy cows.
- **Throw another brain on the barbie**. Meat from a calf younger than three months is called *veal*. Meat

Diagram labels:

Good Tagging Spot
Snout
Chili Meat
Chuck
Rib
Short Ribs
Brisket
Fore Shank
Short Plate Special
Fajita Flank
Knee
Udder
T-Bone
Porterhouse
Pin Bone
Flat Bone
Wedge Bone
Rump
Tip
Tip
Hind Shank
Fly Swatter

from older cattle is *beef*. But the barbecue needn't stop with muscle mass. The heart, kidneys, liver, sweetbreads (pancreas and thymus), testicles, stomach, and tripe (stomach lining) of cattle are also considered finger-licking good.

- **It takes all kinds to make a herd**. There are six main breeds of beef cattle in the United States: Aberdeen-Angus, Brahman, Charolais, Hereford, Polled Hereford, and Simmental.
- **Doin' it**. Heifers are generally mated at 15 months old.
- **In a motherly way**. A bovine pregnancy lasts nine months. At birth a calf weighs from 50 to 100 pounds.
- **Double standard?** Bulls may start breeding at 1 year, but they are usually most active between the ages of 2 and 6.
- **Death salads**. Weeds that may cause illness in cattle: locoweed, death camas, as well as some lupines and larkspurs.
- **Illin'**. Herd diseases affecting cattle: anthrax, blackleg, bloat, brucellosis, foot-and-mouth disease, and mastitis.
- **Cattle census**. In the late 1980s, the Department of Agriculture estimated that there were 102 million head of cattle in the U.S. valued at $41 billion. Texas leads the nation in beef-cattle production. Wisconsin leads the nation in dairy.
- **I'd like to teach the world to moo in perfect harmony**. There are about 1 1/4 billion beef and dairy cattle on Earth. India has more than any other nation, followed by Brazil, the former Soviet Union, and then the United States.
- **Hamburgers, milkshakes, and handbags**. An American eats an average of 75 pounds of beef per year, drinks about 100 quarts of milk, and wears untold millions of pairs of leather weejuns.

covered her wedding bed to be a cozy bedroll for two spread on the floor. Forget about the idea of worming cattle in the morning and browsing department stores in the afternoon. She says that's all a myth. Ranch life then and now centers around cattle in the morning, cattle in the evening, and sometimes cattle all through the night. Shopping? Well, maybe at Christmas.

Unlike Rebecca Gonzales, who hops right in the saddle most mornings, Hallie Stillwell always wore gloves, face powder, and lipstick for cowgirling. Even when the day's schedule called for castrating bulls or checking for screwworms, Hallie fixed her face. Since hers was probably the first saddlebag on the Stillwell Ranch to contain cosmetics, it's not too surprising that Hallie's primping prompted teasing from the other cowhands: "Do you think those cows will notice how you look?" Same goes for Arizona cowgirl and champion trick roper Nancy Kelley Sheppard, who never rides without Elizabeth Arden. "Oh, I've got to have my makeup on all the time. I'm a cowgirl, but no tomboy. My husband still saddles my horse before I ride roundup." For these gals, being a cowgirl never precluded being a lady.

Horses sweat, men perspire, but ladies only glow. When one 1930s cowgirl finally had a bellyfull of such talk, she quipped, "Well, I am working like a horse and I share his privileges."

It's been said that ranching plays hell on women and horses. That rings especially true if the woman runs a ranch, keeps house, and cares for children all at the same time. On today's smaller spreads a woman might function as both cattlewoman and cowgirl, alternately boss and hired hand.

Cowboys and cowgirls seem to have soft spots for the hard life. The average cowhand works five and a half days a week and earns between $9,600 and $12,000 annually plus benefits like housing, health care, and lots of free steak and hamburger. The hours are "dark to dark-thirty," and while they are allowed days off and vacation time, not many ranch hands enjoy a long weekend at the beach. As crazy as it sounds, they'd rather be working.

AGRI-STYLES OF THE RICH & FAMOUS

At Home on the Range with Celebrity Cowpokes

These days, many Beautiful People, bored with conventional conspicuous consumption, are opting to express their individuality through more expansive real-estate purchases. Malibu is so Johnny Carson. Palm Springs so Bob Hope. And Aspen? "Well, you know, I'm not into that scene." Celebrity ranchers buy big in Wyoming and Montana. They don't really spend much time mixing up vaccine or applying bag balm to sore udders, but oh! they look soooooo good in their jeans.

Among the Smart Set paying ranch foremen:

- Tom Brokaw
- Dennis Quaid and Meg Ryan
- Michael Keaton
- Frank Gehry
- Jeff Bridges
- Peter Fonda

- Huey Lewis
- Mel Gibson
- Jane Fonda and Ted Turner
- Melanie Griffith and Don Johnson
- Robert Redford
- Nancy and Ronald Reagan
- Lady Bird Johnson

- Ralph Lauren
- Patrick Swayze
- Sam Donaldson
- Sissy Spacek
- Harrison Ford
- Tommy Lee Jones

It's not unusual for a top hand to work at the same ranch for decades. Loyalty to the land, the cattle, and the brand lies at the heart of the cowpoke's creed. A nimble horse, healthy cattle, and the satisfaction of being tops at a job; as any devoted cowgirl might say, "It just don't git no better 'n that."

Cattlewoman Linda Davis pleads that case eloquently by explaining that she gets restless and itchy when out of the saddle too long. Linda, her husband, Les, and their six children operate a 2,300-head ranch founded by Les's forefathers more than a century ago near Cimarron, New Mexico. Now in her sixties, Linda is involved with various beef boards and cattlemen's organizations, which require lots of travel. In twenty-two months she once racked up more than 100,000 miles on her car, not to mention all the off-road territory covered in her pickup truck with the personalized license tag MRS. BEEF. The whole time she's behind the wheel, Linda says she longs to feel the reins in her hands. She thrives on all the little crises and triumphs of stock work. "That's when I'm really in my element, when I'm riding," she says wistfully. "I regret every single day I'm not at the ranch on a horse."

The cowhand's first love might be her horse, but today her primary transport is more likely to guzzle gas than oats. Since the 1950s, when pickup trucks and other mechanized equipment came into wider usage, ranches began requiring fewer employees. Therefore many small- to medium-sized cattle operations "neighbor" or lend each other hands at roundup time and other crucial junctures during the year.

Twentieth-century cowgirls and cowboys must still display agility on horseback to excel in their field, but today they tend to spend more time driving all-terrain vehicles than spurring horses. And one helicopter can do the work of many cowboys if it's piloted by a woman or a man who can think like a cow. The hired hands on a modern cattle ranch might wear paging devices or have cellular phones in their saddlebags. After ten or so hours of getting little dogies along, a 1990s cowgirl drives home to microwave some supper and watch satellite TV. Long gone are the days of spearing a bean by the campfire and counting the stars.

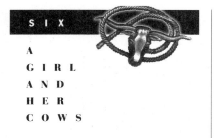

Ranch chores change with the seasons, and the seasonal cycle varies considerably from region to region. Typically, the winter months mean feeding time. Since the grass doesn't nourish as thoroughly as in spring and summer, the cowgirl's main cold-weather task is to supply hay or cattle cake to her herds for extra nutrition. In some areas, calves are born in late winter; in other parts of the country the little ones arrive in early summer. March and April bring roundup time. Ranch workers gather all the stock into pens for branding, vaccinating, and castrating. During the summer months, the stock is back in the pasture, where the rich grass usually eliminates the need for extra feeding. When the leaves begin to change, it's roundup time once again. After the fall roundup, the crew culls the steers and heifers bound for market (some operations sell cow-calf pairs instead) from the rest of the herd.

Saturday morning in tiny Muleshoe, Texas, ranchers gather at the auction house to bid on pigs, horses, and cows. Before the sale commences indoors, browsers outside the sale hall climb steps to rickety wooden catwalks spanning the cattle pens below. From this perch cowgirls and cowboys gaze down on the bawling bovine buffet, picking out livestock in the same way they'd choose an entrée at the cafeteria. One man scribbles notes in a little book. A woman points out a particularly nice-looking heifer to her husband. Later when the bidding begins she'll raise her hand to make a buy offer.

In ranching areas, weekend auctions like this one are long-standing rituals. But they're not the only way to buy or sell a cow. Another marketing method involves contracting a number of animals to a single buyer earlier in the year, then shipping directly to him for more feeding and eventual slaughter. Cows also go on the block through video auction, in which buyers peruse stock via VCR. Regardless of how they're sold, once a load of beef-on-the-hoof leaves the ranch, the seasonal cycle begins all over again.

Call cows the alpha, but never the omega, of the ranching industry. Some herds go baaa instead of moo. Still others oink or bleat. Patti Stickler's cash crop makes hardly any noise at all. She raises ostriches in Oklahoma and calls the big bird's high-protein, low-cholesterol red meat the "health food of the future." Texas bird

TAKE THIS JOB AND LOVE IT

A Day in the Life of the Modern Cowgirl

5:30 AM: The alarm clock screams. The cowgirl's feet hit the floor before her eyes fully open. She grabs a cup of coffee. Loads the pickup with bales of hay.

6:00: She drives to the back pasture—careful not to spill too much coffee while going over bumps. Locates the herd. Unloads one bale at a time to supplement the stock's grass diet.

7:00: Puts Cap'n Crunch on the table for the children's breakfast. Gives them lunch money. Sends them off to the school-bus stop.

8:00: In the barn, a cow is about to deliver a calf. The cowgirl pulls on a rubber glove and checks the position of the not-yet-born baby.

11:00: Back at the trailer for lunch—bologna on white bread with mayonnaise, Chee-tos, soda—in front of the television.

Noon: The heat of the day is too hot to work. Soap operas offer a modern siesta alternative.

1:00 PM: After *Loving* and *All My Children,* the cowgirl is back in the barn shoeing two horses from the ranch's remuda.

2:15: While she's horseshoeing—the ends of the nails sticking out of her mouth, hammer in one hand, the horse's hoof clutched between her knees—a neighboring rancher stops in to look over a bull he's thinking of buying.

2:30: She shows the bull and gossips with the prospective buyer, then returns to the horseshoeing.

3:10: She saddles her horse and practices her roping technique for an upcoming weekend competition.

3:45: The phone rings. She runs to the trailer, but not in time.

The cowgirl doesn't believe in answering machines.

4:00: The children get home. She takes them along in the pickup for one last look at the herd.

5:30: She nukes four frozen Mexican dinners for her family's supper.

6:15: She sits down at her desk, pays bills, looks over stock records, makes a few phone calls. While the cowgirl attempts to calculate how much vaccine to order, she's interrupted four times by her daughter saying, "Mommy, look. Look, mommy. Look at me."

7:30: She spends ten minutes watching Reba on The Nashville Network.

8:00: She helps her husband get the children to bed.

8:10: She returns to her ledgers.

9:00: She argues with her husband about whether or not *Roseanne* is a positive role model.

9:10: They kiss and make up, agreeing to disagree.

9:30: They continue to make up.

10:00: She pops open a beer and plops down on the sofa to watch *Studs*.

10:30: She picks up a tabloid from the coffee table. Reads an article about an eighty-year-old woman who gave birth to triplets. Wishes such miracles would happen to her cows.

11:00: She takes off her boots. Brushes her teeth, and climbs into bed, one tired buckaroo.

5:00 AM: The alarm clock screams. The cowgirl's feet hit the floor before her eyes fully open. She grabs a cup of coffee . . .

rancher Pat Sutton deals a similar boast about emu steak, adding "it tastes a lot like veal." In Pennsylvania, Caroline Kressly produces llamas on her ranch. Louisiana alligator farmer Sandra Montoucet's amphibious herd graze in the bayou. At La Coma Ranch near the Texas-Mexico border, Marge Bentsen, her husband and three daughters wrangle rhino. Yep, a rhinoceros ranch.

Then there's Sister Mary Bernadette Muller, the cowgirl nun. She and some of her cloistered Franciscan colleagues operate a small-horse ranch in central Texas. "Small-horse ranch" means they raise miniature, lap-sized horses at the Monastery of Saint Clare. Sister Bernadette and her diminutive four-legged friends attract busloads of tourists each year. They've even been featured on the *CBS Evening News*. The uplifting and slightly comic sight of the cowgirl clerics,

with their dusty cowboy boots peeking out from beneath the skirts of traditional nuns' habits, made even frosty Dan Rather smile.

Reptile ranching. Rabbit ranching. Rhino ranching. What's next, hamster ranching? All too often the word "ranch" (from the Spanish *rancho*, meaning livestock farm) gets tossed around where it shouldn't. You might see signs for the Waterbed Ranch on the freeway for example, or think twice about a shampoo and blow dry at the Hair Ranch Salon. The movie and Broadway musical *The Best Little Whorehouse in Texas* sprang from the true story of a now defunct place called the Chicken Ranch, which sold neither eggs nor fryers.

THE COWGIRL POET

Old Vogal

By Peggy Godfrey

Told me I was lucky
When I went to cut his hay
A bloom or two means lots of leaves
'Course it's best that way.

He assured me I was lucky
That my bales were done up tight
Lucky that I caught the dew
And chanced to bale it right.

Oh, yes, and I was lucky
When storm clouds came around
All my hay was in a stack
Not layin' on the ground.

I clenched my jaw and held my tongue
Red anger 'round me swirled
If I'z a man he'd say I'z good
But "LUCKY" 'cuz I'm a girl.

Whether it's crocodiles or cows, ranching affords plenty of job perks. A ranch woman can be her own boss, set her own hours, work at home and be near her family. The dress code is casual, very casual. No high heels, no panty hose, makeup optional. A cowgirl can even go to the office without first brushing her teeth, just as long as it doesn't offend the cows.

Ranching has its down sides as well. Money, for one. Most any cattleman or cattlewoman will advise the greenhorn to consider real estate or law or anything but a cattle career, especially if a bank account with lots of digits ranks as a primary goal. Ranch life can get lonely too. The hours drag long, and it's a rare cowgirl who hasn't kept an all-night vigil during calving season. The working conditions often stack up as less than ideal—heat, cold, rain, snow. And some of the tasks a rancher undertakes are unpleasant, to say the least.

A woman chooses ranching because she fancies the feel of a good horse moving after cows. She likes the dramatic sweep of a big horizon and finds comfort in the certainty of a mother cow caring for her newborn calf. A cowgirl rides herd because she believes herself to be a small part of a bigger, grander scheme. Ranching, you see, is more than a career; it's a calling. Those who do it, do it for the love of the job.

CHAPTER SEVEN

SHARPSHOOTING, TRICK ROPING, AND YODELING LOVE SONGS

O.K. Great idea for a TV sit-com. Kind of The Partridge Family *meets* Bonanza *with a* Designing Women *kind of feeling. Trust me. You're gonna love this. See, there are these three attractive young women—and, uh—their pet dog. Scene opens as they lounge around the living room of a ranch-style house in—let's just say in suburban Dallas. With me so far? O.K., so like the decor of this place is that real cowboy campy look, you know? Hmmm—I see a leather sofa, some Native American art and horseshoes and branding irons, all that rancho neat-o stuff hanging on the walls. Wide shot on the women, right? They're talking, laughing, swigging Cokes from those*

small green bottles. Then a tight shot on one of the girls wearing cowboy boots and jodhpurs or something. She sort of casually picks up a guitar and drawls real spontaneous like, "Hey, yew all, I've got an idea for a li'l ol' song." Then…

SOUNDS LIKE something already in development out in Hollywood, right? Well, don't touch that dial. It's no sitcom. The cowgirl is alive and well and picking and grinning and yodeling love songs in North Dallas. Not just one cowgirl, but three of them—Laura Lynch and two sisters,

S H A R P -
S H O O T I N G ,
T R I C K
R O P I N G ,
A N D
Y O D E L I N G
L O V E

Martie and Emily Erwin—have formed a band called the Dixie Chicks. They tout themselves as "nightingales of the prairie." Through their two record albums, live performances, and TV commercials for McDonald's, they've gained a cult following by blowing new life into traditional western swing.

The "henhouse" where the Dixie Chicks rehearse, their clothes, their personalities, and their music come across as pure cowgirl, even

The Dixie Chicks.

DRAWL OR TWANG?

A Word About Western Diction

A Clip 'n' Save Guide to Talkin' Cowgirl

"You're from Tennessee, right?" A bartender in New York City asked a Texas cowgirl. "I love your drawl."

The cowgirl fumed. "You deaf or somethin'? This is no dang drawl. I'm talkin' to you with a big ol' twang. Tennessee? Hell, no. You're hearin' Texas right here, buddy. T-E-X-A-S. I'm talkin' Texas."

They're not the same, you know—the drawl and the twang. But sometimes they come together. The difference has lots to do with diphthongs and fricatives and glottal stops. But for nonlinguists, the shorter explanation: Drawl is slow speech with prolonged vowels, and it is associated with the South. The twang sounds more nasal and is associated more with the West.

If you want to talk like a cowgirl, by all means do it right. There's nothing more annoying than a city slicker trying to be cute by saying "you all" when she means "y'all." Clip out these eight little rules. Put them in your purse for quick reference before taking your prairie accent public.

- **Rule 1**. Stretch words. Just grab a vowel sound and pull that sucker out as far as it'll go. EXAMPLE: *"All right*! Now he is naked" becomes *"Awriiiiiight*! Now, he's nekid."

- **Rule 2**. Substitute "fixing to" for "preparing to." EXAMPLE: "I'm *preparing* to hit you" becomes "I'm *fixin'* to kick your butt."

- **Rule 3**. Drop the "g" from "ing" words. EXAMPLE: "I'm fixin' to go ridin'."

- **Rule 4**. Say "git" for "get." And remember that "git" can be a synonym for "scram." EXAMPLE: "I'm tired of lookin' at y'all—*git*!"

- **Rule 5**. Liberally sprinkle sentences with "big ol'." EXAMPLE: "She was drivin' this *big ol'* fat boy around town in a *big ol'* Cadillac."

- **Rule 6**. Throw in folksy axioms whenever possible. EXAMPLE: "She wasn't very bright" becomes "She was a coupla sandwiches shy of a picnic."

- **Rule 7**. Never, ever say "oil business" when you mean "awl bidness." EXAMPLE: "Daddy did a little bidness down here, *awl bidness*."

- **Rule 8**. "Ma'am" and "sir"—use them to death. All women are "ma'am" and all men are "sir" regardless of age. EXAMPLE: "Yes, ma'am, it's time for you to kiss Mommy and go night-night."

SEVEN

SHARP-
SHOOTING,
TRICK
ROPING,
AND
YODELING
LOVE
SONGS

if their bios do not. Emily Erwin learned to play the violin at age seven, picked up the banjo three years later, and joined the Dixie Chicks while still in high school. Emily's big sister, Martie, has played classical violin since kindergarten and bluegrass fiddle since junior high. Bass player Laura Lynch actually did grow up on a cattle ranch. Forsaking the prairie for Wall Street, she spent a few years wheeling and dealing as a stockbroker before returning to her rural roots through music.

Each of the band members looks as if she'd be more comfortable behind the wheel of a Volvo station wagon than astride a cow pony. However, the group's smooth harmonies and their good-natured yodeling on tunes like "I Want to Be a Cowboy's Sweetheart" suggest that these gals are cowgirls in the truest Dale Evans tradition.

Even though Laura is the only one of the group who earned her cowgirl credentials by branding calves and herding cows, the Dixie Chicks represent the latest chapter in a book that began with the first show-business cowgirl, Annie Oakley, and continued with rodeo stunt riders and gals in sparkling outfits twirling rope tricks at county fairs.

Today, cowgirl performers might turn up anywhere around the world—from Wild West shows to movies to TV to radio to concert halls to advertising billboards. Modern-day show-biz buckaroos like the Dixie Chicks are part of a trend. Although not cowgirls by vocation, this bunch acquired the label via attitude, style, and spirit. No horse, no cows, just cute costumes and buttery harmonies. Call the Dixie Chicks urban cowgirls or drugstore cowgirls or all-hat-and-no-cattle cowgirls. Just be sure to call them cowgirls.

Each evening not too far from the Eiffel Tower, Annie Oakley and Buffalo Bill teach Europeans a thing or two about the West. These days, Bill and Annie work their magic in a dazzling western-themed circus at Euro Disney, the American theme park near Paris. The current production marks the latest Continental run of Buffalo Bill's Wild West Show and the first in almost a century.

Buffalo Bill? Annie Oakley? Still performing? Still breathing? Well, sort of. The original Bill and Annie were long ago called to the Final Roundup, so today actors reprise their roles. Texas cowgirl

Sonna Warvell, the Annie Oakley of the 1990s.

Sonna Warvell is one of two American women hired portraying Annie Oakley.

Sonna Warvell is no newcomer to cowgirling or entertainment. Several decades ago, her mother gained a modicum of fame in a cowgirl act called "Arena Kachina & White Feather" in which she jumped a bareback horse, without reins or bridle, over a convertible. When she was a girl, Sonna and her sister joined their parent's act, performing trick-riding and trick-roping exhibitions at rodeos, cir-

SEVEN

SHARP-
SHOOTING,
TRICK
ROPING,
AND
YODELING
LOVE
SONGS

cuses, and fairs all over the United States, and in Brazil and Singapore. When not roping for an audience, Sonna helped her father lasso calves at home in Weatherford, Texas.

A roping contest among show cowboys is part of the Euro Disney Wild West. One night, when Sonna wasn't scheduled to perform, she put on a fake beard, dressed up like a guy, entered the contest and won. Although she does some fancy shooting and riding as Annie Oakley, Sonna says, "Trick roping has always been my thing."

"My dad and Annie Oakley were born in the same place—Darke County, Ohio. And I've always sort of identified with her," Sonna says. "Brave, confident, glamorous, famous—she was all things little girls dream of being when they grow up."

Disney's Wild West show duplicates the extravaganza William F. "Buffalo Bill" Cody brought to life in the 1880s. It begins flashback-style with Buffalo Bill reminiscing about his first Continental tour. Then the entertainment proceeds in much the same way the original show did a hundred years ago: real cowboys and genuine American Indians ride and shoot and rope and paint an exciting picture of life in wild territory. The modern show is more streamlined than the original. Since the troupe doesn't travel, there's no need to haul buffalo and livestock across the ocean or over mountain ranges. Two different actors play Sitting Bull. There are a couple of Buffalo Bills on the payroll too—and a matched set of Annie Oakleys. Missouri native Cheryl Lawson, a former rodeo trick rider and film actress, brings Annie to life on stage on alternate evenings—she and Sonna split the role.

The modern version of the Wild West show is dinner theater. The audience chomps on barbecue ribs and scarfs down beans while Annie Oakley shoots and Buffalo Bill brags about his bravery. In their living quarters near the park, fifty American cowboys and cowgirls drink café au lait and eat croissants for breakfast in much the same way Buffalo Bill's original cast did during the cowboys' first conquest of Europe. When cast members in their western garb stroll down the Champs-Élysées they get funny looks from passersby. Sometimes the other pedestrians make comments like "Howdy, cowboy" in thick French accents.

PITCHMEN O' THE PRAIRIE

Cowpokes on Madison Avenue

Tom Mix sold Ralston cereal products on the radio in the 1930s. Gene Autry peddled Wrigley gum through the airwaves.Roy Rogers sold Quaker Oats, Dodge cars, and later roast-beef sandwiches.

The cowpoke is alive and well and busy on Madison Avenue even today. *The New York Times* advertising columnist Stuart Elliott sees the cowboy as a kind of shorthand. "Advertisers use them to tap into the spirit of adventure hidden inside consumers"; the cowboy/cowgirl ideal appeals to our images of our best selves.

On the tube, on billboards beside the freeway, and in all sorts of magazines, images of cowboys and cowgirls are used to sell:

- Guess jeans
- Stetson cologne
- Hanes T-shirts
- Wrangler jeans
- Pringle's potato chips
- Luke Perry
- Pace picante sauce
- Marlboro cigarettes
- Mazda automobiles
- Ford trucks
- Coors beer
- Ebel wristwatches
- The Ralph Lauren lifestyle
- Ronald Reagan
- Roy Rogers roast-beef sandwiches
- Bounty paper towels
- Kellogg's Rice Krispies
- Squirt soft drinks

Coca-Cola advertisement, 1937.

SEVEN

SHARP-
SHOOTING,
TRICK
ROPING,
AND
YODELING
LOVE
SONGS

Sonna Warvell says Europeans love cowgirls. "I don't know if the show would be so popular back in the States. At home people kind of take cowgirls and cowboys for granted. Over here, folks halfway believe that everybody in America rides a horse and wears a Stetson."

In Tom Robbins's novel *Even Cowgirls Get the Blues*, a character called Bonanza Jellybean bemoans a puzzling paradox. She complains: "So they let you dress up like a cowgirl, and when you say, 'I'm gonna be a cowgirl when I grow up,' they laugh and say, 'Ain't she cute.' Then one day they tell you, 'Look, honey, cowgirls are only play. You can't *really* be one.'"

There's a grain of truth in this gal's gripe. In a sense, show business converted cowgirl from honest occupation to mere costume. For decades, images of Annie Oakley and Dale Evans have replaced notions of weathered women on horseback in many American minds whenever the word "cowgirl" is spoken. But pity the fool who might try to tell the characters in the movie *Thelma and Louise* that cowgirls don't really exist. Barreling through the desert, dodging the law, Thelma and Louise looked mighty authentic—real rough, tough Western heroines. When Louise trades her jewelry for a hat to keep the sun off her face, and throws her lipstick away, she illustrates a point: These days a cowgirl isn't just a starlet wearing a fringy miniskirt, she's a formidable force to be reckoned with, a no-fooling American Amazon.

Modern-day movie cowgirls don't necessarily always strut their stuff out West either. In the *Alien* trilogy, the heroine confronts fierce natives on another lawless frontier—outer space. A pistol-packing cosmic cowgirl fights the futuristic bad guys of the *Terminator* movies. Catwoman, from *Batman Returns*, does her cowgirling with claws and a whip in lawless Gotham City. Those flicks might not fit the *High Noon* western mold, but whether the drama is set on the Great Plains or on Mars, the leading female characters of modern cinema are often cowgirls—strong women making the best of difficult situations.

Actress and fitness guru Jane Fonda does the more traditional cowgirl thing. She and husband Ted Turner own a ranch in Montana, where they raise buffalo. Sissy Spacek raises horses in Virginia. Angelica Houston plays the cowgirl role too—off camera most of the time.

Actresses may be wearing boots and riding wild horses in real life, but parts for conventional Old West cowgirls on the big screen haven't come along too often. In fact, throughout the history of film, cowboys, not cowgirls, have grabbed most of the cinematic glory.

While the Wild West shows were still touring the country, the

THE HORSE OPERA HALL OF FAME

Classic Cowgirl Cinema

- The Outlaw
- The Misfits
- Giant
- Honky Tonk
- Destry Rides Again
- Trouble in Texas
- Calamity Jane
- Cat Ballou
- Rooster Cogburn
- True Grit

- Johnny Guitar
- The Cattle Queen of Montana
- Annie Oakley
- Annie Get Your Gun
- Girl Crazy
- Western Girls
- Rowdy Ann
- The Singing Cowgirl
- The Big Country
- Oklahoma!

- The Girl of the Golden West
- Duel in the Sun
- Aliens (trilogy)
- The Unsinkable Molly Brown
- Thelma & Louise
- Terminator (1 and 2)
- The Cowboy and the Senorita
- A League of Their Own
- 9 to 5
- Coal Miner's Daughter

THE COWGIRL POET

Thank Heavens for Dale Evans

By Martie Erwin,
Robin Lynn Macy,
and Lisa Brandenburg
(as recorded by the Dixie Chicks)

I grew up on Bob Wills and daydreams
My toes were a-tappin' to western swing
I wished upon a star
Atop an old boxcar
Chasing rainbows to the place the bluebirds sing!
I painted my eyes up like Dolly
Sang with Kitty Wells 'til momma screamed
Then daddy shook his head as he carried me to bed
And tucked me in a-beggin' me to sing:

Thank Heavens for Dale Evans
You're everything I ever want to be
Yodel-lay-ee, Yodel-lay-ee,

Yodel-lay-ee
Dale Evans made a cowgirl out of me.

Now I play my guitar with the cowgirls
And what I got they never bat an eye
Like Shirley Temple's curls
Thank heavens for the girls
We'll sing a song to make a cowboy cry!
I never got the limo or the diamond
But I got my hat, my boots and my guitar
I'm proud enough to say
I'll always be this way
Like the girl who went and stole Roy Rogers' heart.

cowboy rode into Hollywood. In 1898, the Edison Company produced the first western movie, *Cripple Creek Barroom*. That silent film was little more than a skit performed in costume as cameras rolled, but it portended bigger and better things to follow. In 1903, with the first blush still clinging to movie technology, came *The Great Train Robbery*, a picture audiences found so realistic that some people fainted during screenings.

During the 1920s cinema cowboys started talking. By the 1930s they were singing as well. But not kissing. Never randy, crime-fighting wranglers had no time for romance on screen. Even so, Americans ate up movie westerns with the same gusto with which they had gobbled dime novels and Wild West shows. Tom Mix, Hoot Gibson, Gene Autry, Hopalong Cassidy, Roy Rogers—a whole posse of cowboy stars emerged.

Such big business were westerns that Tom Mix built a minitown called Mixville between Hollywood and Santa Monica to expedite movie making. Cast and crew members lived in bunkhouses and cottages on the grounds of Mixville during filmings. A full-scale replica of a frontier town made suitable sets for shooting exterior as well interior scenes. Movie-trained cattle and horses grazed nearby, and Mix even kept a collection of stagecoaches, buggies, and covered wagons as standby props. Simply add a script and Mixville became a one-stop shop for western-movie making.

Moguls churned out low-budget assembly-line western movies at quite a clip, often finishing an entire picture in only a few days. The scripts of these so-called B-westerns relied on tried and true formulaic plots, which always involved a good-guy star helping law enforcers track down dastardly bad-guy killers or rustlers. The stories rarely varied, and the cowboy's horse was always his most trusted ally. Equine co-stars such as Roy Rogers's mount, Trigger—"The Smartest Horse in the Movies"—and Gene Autry's four-legged friend, Champion—"The World's Wonder Horse"—always got billing above the female lead.

Many of the B-western cowboys migrated to Hollywood from ranches by way of Wild West shows. Cowgirls recognized an opening

SEVEN

S H A R P -
S H O O T I N G ,
T R I C K
R O P I N G ,
A N D
Y O D E L I N G
L O V E
S O N G S

there too, although not one big enough to stampede through. A number of cowgirls ditched the rodeo or Wild West life in search of movie stardom. Few found it. Helen Gibson, the wife of cowboy star Hoot Gibson, made the cut. When her job with Miller Brothers 101 Ranch Wild West Show played out and left her stranded in California in 1911, Helen's good looks and riding ability landed her work in the movies. Each morning she rode her horse from her home in Venice to Topango Canyon, where many early westerns were shot. Her pay: eight dollars a week.

Not all cowgirls who moved out to Hollywood ended up smiling for the camera. Ability to handle a horse could be as valuable as acting skill on the coast and some gals made money as wranglers or stock handlers. Other former Wild West and rodeo hands became stunt riders for the movies. Broncobuster Bertha Blancett took falls for Bison Moving Picture Company in the 1910s. Rodeo star Vera

McGinnis also found work as a stunt woman about that same time. Once, when doubling for the female lead in a picture, Vera was directed to fall from a running horse. The shot required five takes, and she collected $10 each time she hit the dirt.

Almost every actress imaginable played some variety of western woman. Lana Turner starred opposite Clark Gable in *Honky Tonk*. Rita Hayworth paid her B-western dues in *Trouble in Texas*. *Destry Rides Again* featured sultry Marlene Dietrich. Doris Day sang and danced the starring role in *Calamity Jane*. Katharine Hepburn worked opposite John Wayne in *Rooster Cogburn*. Jane Fonda played cowgirl in *Cat Ballou*. Joan Crawford appeared in several westerns: *The Law of the Range*, *Johnny Guitar*, and a musical, *Montana Moon*, among others. Barbara Stanwyck got comfortable in her cowgirl costume as well. Her four big-screen westerns included *Annie Oakley* and *The Cattle Queen of Montana*. Then there was a whole herd of actresses who played cowgirl sidekicks to the cowboys stars, most notably Dale Evans.

Even during the 1970s, with such films as *Butch Cassidy and the Sundance Kid*, *McCabe and Mrs. Miller*, *Paint Your Wagon*, and *The Outlaw Josey Wales*, women remained scenery in western movies. Except for *Urban Cowboy*, which spawned a brief mechanical-bull-riding craze, and *Silverado*, cowboy pictures all but disappeared during the 1980s. Hollywood heroines of the Reagan era were

southern belles, not cowgirls. In *Broadcast News*, *Terms of Endearment*, and *Steel Magnolias*, the strong women spoke with a southern drawl.

When the western finally slipped back into theaters, the recipe had changed. Academy Award winner *Dances with Wolves* worked as sort of a reverse western, in which the Indians played the good guys. The comedy *City Slickers* centered around touchy-feely men exploring their more emotional sides during a cattle drive, and it did gangbuster business at the box office. A traditional shoot 'em up western, *Young Guns*, flopped in theaters. Modern moviegoers seemed to be shopping for something new and different.

Western movies got a shot of estrogen. Among the toughest, most popular movie cowboys of the 1990s rode several cowgirlish women. Critics likened the main characters in *Thelma and Louise* to Butch and Sundance. Others called the film a "women's buddy picture," unusual not only in offering the primary roles to cowgirls in spirit, but also in relegating the cowboy-types to supporting parts. Films like *Thelma and Louise* have cleaned away the goopy makeup from the cowgirl image, and given young cowgirl wannabes hope: Look, honey, cowgirls are *not* only play. You *can* really be one.

When Jeanna Clare glides her Coupe de Ville convertible to a stop at the extra-unleaded pump, service-station employees seldom raise their heads from the oil-change or full-service fill-up of the moment. The guy cleaning the windshield pays little attention to Jeanna's outfit—a vintage 1950s cowgirl getup with a fringed skirt and vest, boots, and a hat held securely atop her curls by a little string chin strap. After all, this is Texas; when Jeanna cruises in, the guys with the chamois cloths just politely wave and go on about the big business of caring for big cars.

Jeanna Clare, aged sixty something, made her mark as a television cowgirl during the 1960s. And thanks to public-access cable TV, her career continues today through videotaped reruns. In the passenger seat of Jeanna's Cadillac rides her partner, Don Mahoney. He's dapper in a ten-gallon hat and a Tom Mix-cut polyester suit to match

SHARP-
SHOOTING,
TRICK
ROPING,
AND
YODELING
LOVE
SONGS

Jeanna's ensemble. For years the duo starred in *Don Mahoney and Jeanna Clare with Their Kiddie Troopers*—a down-home children's talent show best described as part *Captain Kangaroo*, part *Hee Haw*.

Don and Jeanna indirectly attribute the continuing popularity of their show to Don's friend Al Jolson. "He once told me that if you use four things you will always be successful in show business," Don explains. "You work with kids, wave the flag, have something to do with animals, or have something to do about mother. Well, our television show set is an old hay barn with an old water barrel, and on the wall is an American flag. We ride in on horses and have mothers as guests. So we followed his good advice."

Don came to TV during the late 1940s after a brief career in what he calls "C" westerns. He appeared as a singing cowboy in *Deadman's Gold, Song of the West,* and *Blazing Gun* before he began losing his eyesight. One motion-picture producer suggested he could make Don the greatest, richest western star in the world through a series of movies about "The Blind Cowboy and His Seeing-Eye Horse." But Don had other, more tasteful ideas for himself. With his vision fading, he headed home to Texas and television.

Soon he was doing six live television shows per week. He'd fly to Lubbock for a show one day (where young Buddy Holly was once a guest), then off to Fort Worth the next day (where Elvis appeared on the show), then on to San Antonio and Beaumont and back to Houston.

If any cowboy needs a sidekick, a blind cowboy does. In 1956 with his eyesight almost gone, Don moseyed up to the snack bar in the Beaumont airport and said howdy to a talented country girl with a big-city voice. The young lady introduced herself as Dido Rowley. Before long Dido dressed up in cowgirl outfits to match Don's flashy duds and became his TV saddle pal. "Don Mahoney with His Kiddie Troopers" became "Don Mahoney and Jeanna Clare with Their Kiddie Troopers" and a permanent partnership began.

"I changed her name to Jeanna Clare," Don says, "'Don and Dido' just didn't sound right. I wanted her to use the name Clare somehow because you know Saint Clare is the patron saint of television and I thought that would be lucky." Even back then, Don and Jeanna could see that television was the prairie for the modern cowpoke to ride.

Don Mahoney and Jeanna Clare and Their Kiddie Troopers.

SEVEN

SHARP-
SHOOTING,
TRICK
ROPING,
AND
YODELING
LOVE
SONGS

Don Mahoney stepped straight from the big screen to the small one. But other movie cowboys conquered the ether before trying TV. The radio cowboy of the 1930s had a simple twofold mission: to offer hope to the people of the Depression, and to express to young listeners the cowboy credo of patriotism, law, order, truth, justice, and bold action. *The Tom Mix Radio Show* went on the air in 1933 and carried the moral message that "straight shooters" like Tom and his pals always win. Writers deliberately patterned the radio character the Lone Ranger after the G-men of the era, who stomped bootlegging hoods like Al Capone. So great was the Lone Ranger's popularity with young radio listeners that when the Detroit Symphony Orchestra launched into a rendition of the masked horseman's theme, "The William Tell Overture," during a 1937 performance, a child in the audience leaped up and shouted, "Hi-yo, Silver, away!"

The Lone Ranger wasn't actually all that lone. Another cowboy do-gooder called Red Ryder also carried the same God-and-country message to young America. Then there was the Cisco Kid. And Gene Autry: his weekly radio half-hour on CBS, *Melody Ranch*, went on the air in 1940. If the radio cowboys of the 1930s were intended as metaphors for G-men fighting gangsters, the 1940s radio heroes combated Axis surrogates and sold a good deal more than patriotism while they were at it. Tom Mix hawked Ralston cereal on the air, and his picture appeared on product boxes. When Quaker Oats sponsored Roy Rogers's radio show, a commercial jingle promised listeners a cereal "delicious, nutritious, makes you ambitious."

Roy Rogers's sales didn't stop with oats. His movie, radio, and later television stardom spawned a merchandising industry. On the air, Roy lent his name to Goodyear and Quaker Oaks and Dodge, and on department store shelves his likeness decorated lunch boxes, flashlights, pocket knives and scores of other toys and collectibles. But Roy didn't corner the cowboy market. Little boys of the radio and early-television era drooled for the Hopalong Cassidy bicycle with "genuine leather holsters" mounted on the handlebars. They whined for a pair of authentic Gene Autry galoshes, or begged mom for a Tom Mix Straight Shooter ring. Along with the ring came the Straight

Shooter Manual featuring the "Tom Mix Chart of Wounds," a nifty map of the hero's twelve bullet scars and forty-seven bone fractures.

Little girls liked cowboy stuff too. A story was circulated during the 1950s about a woman who promised her daughter a visit from

June Storey, Gene Autry, and Patsy Montana.

CHEATIN', GETTIN' DRUNK, AND LOVIN' THE WRONG MAN

Patsy Montana's Tips on How to Write a Country Song

"Lying here with Gene Autry on my mind," might have made an appropriate chorus for Patsy Montana's first hit record. Patsy was thinking about Gene when she wrote the ground-breaking country classic "I Want to Be a Cowboy's Sweetheart" in the early 1930s.

"Back then there weren't many girl singers in Nashville, so there weren't many girls' songs," Patsy says. "I just wrote my own." Since then this prolific singing cowgirl has published more than two hundred tunes and recorded nine albums. She can write a song from start to finish in half an hour if her creative juices are flowing just right. Other times, a catchy phrase or ditty will roll around in her head for years without fully fermenting. Patsy believes songwriting is something of a God-given talent, and she modestly insists that she's more of a singer who writes songs than a songwriter who sings. Each writer works differently, but the Montana Method goes something like this:

- **Step 1**: The Title. Patsy begins at the very beginning. Sometimes a catchy phrase just leaps out at her. "When I Get Time," for example, is a Patsy title currently waiting to be coupled with a tune. Another work-in-progress is "All Boy and Smile Wide." What does it mean? Patsy's not entirely sure just yet, she simply likes the way the words work together.

Many country songs feature women as victims, victims of a two-timin' husband, too many snot-nosed children, poverty, depression, and D-I-V-O-R-C-E. No such pitiful Pearls populate Patsy's music. Favorite themes of hers include life in the wide-open spaces and cowgirl romance—"I've never written about stay-at-home gals waiting for a man, but about tomboys not afraid to go after what they want."

- **Step 2**: The Chorus. Once Patsy has settled on a title, she starts shaping the chorus by expanding on the original phrase, and perhaps adding a few measures of Nashville-style yodeling.

- **Step 3**: The Tune. This part separates the songwriting women from the girls. Sometimes the tune emerges piece-of-cake right along with the title and the chorus. Other times the creative well runs dry. Tunes have jumped from Patsy's subconscious to her conscious while she's sleeping, when she's driving, or watching TV. Fusing the words and the music can sometimes be mix-and-match.

"You know I'll have a few good tunes I've been unable to find words for, and a snappy chorus or two without music so I just try to tack 'em together and see what happens."

Hopalong Cassidy on her birthday if the child would take her medicine and say her prayers every day. The girl did as her mother asked, and when birthday time approached the mother frantically wrote Hoppy explaining her predicament: Could he at least send her daughter a card? The cowboy star did one better, and showed up for the Hoppy birthday party, where little girls were eating cake from Hoppy paper plates on a Hoppy tablecloth with Hoppy napkins and wishing the honoree many Hoppy returns on the day.

Connoisseurs of cowgirl memorabilia had a tougher time scoring neat-o merchandise. While never as collectible as a Ted Williams rookie card, or even an issue of a Roy Rogers comic book, sets of cowgirl postcards featuring B-western buckaroos were issued during the 1940s and 1950s. The Bradley Time Company manufactured a Queen of the West Dale Evans wristwatch. And Dale starred in her own series of comic-book adventures between 1948 and 1959. In the colored panels of the comics Dale delivered robbers and rustlers to the sheriff without any help from Roy.

Comics and radio weren't the only ways to drop in on Roy and Dale at the Double-Bar-R. Boys and girls lucky enough to live in homes with television sets could also watch the King of the Cowboys and the Queen of the West on TV beginning in the early 1950s. For television, Roy portrayed a California rancher. Dale Evans and Pat Brady acted as his human sidekicks. Trigger, Dale's horse Buttermilk, and Bullet, "The Wonder Dog," rounded out the all-mammal ensemble cast.

The Double-Bar-R wasn't the only cattle operation on prime time. The all-male Cartwright family of *Bonanza* lived on the Ponderosa. Other Old West television western programs showcased law enforcers such as Marshal Matt Dillon of *Gunsmoke*, Wyatt Earp of *Wyatt Earp*, bounty hunter Josh Randal of *Wanted—Dead or Alive*, and the early U.S. intelligence agent Jim West in *The Wild Wild West*.

The prime-time lineups of the 1970s included programs about cowboys of the New West. Matt Houston cut a dapper figure as a modern-day cowboy-style private investigator in an eponymous series. Sam McCloud of *McCloud* sleuthed in a Stetson too. Horse opera met soap opera on *Dallas* where the feuds and lurid romantic entanglements of the Ewings at South Fork Ranch were a good deal more racy than any action Roy and Dale ever undertook back at the Double-Bar-R.

Gunslingers, Prairie Madonnas, hookers with hearts of gold, bimbos in sunbonnets—cowgirls of some sort have long been present in prime time. Gene Autry's production company filmed eighty episodes of *Annie Oakley* for television during the 1950s. On *The Big Valley*, Barbara Stanwyck portrayed a Prairie Madonna type. Miss Kitty of *Gunsmoke*, played by Amanda Blake, came across as a saloon keeper with a Christian conscience. Stefanie Powers once did a *Bonanza* guest spot as Calamity Jane, and a bevy of marriage-hungry bubbleheads chased the handsome male stars on *Here Come the Brides*.

From this pantheon of western women in televisionland, however, no true cowgirl heroine emerged. And by the time female-centered programs like *Cagney and Lacey* and *Designing Women* came around, America seemed to have lost interest in the Old West. Today network lineups boast many strong, multifaceted female characters, but the world still awaits its first cowgirl sitcom.

That doesn't mean cowboys and cowgirls have become old hat to television viewers. Recently, Old West TV trotted bashfully back into vogue. Anonymous cowgirls grace the tube in thirty-second doses, selling everything from potato chips to cologne. In network prime time, *The Young Riders* centers around the lives of a pony express crew. Children born a full generation too late for Roy Rogers laughed at the antics of Cowboy Curtis on *Pee-Wee's Playhouse*. Another Saturday-morning show for children features a singing group, Riders in the Sky, doing the job of Mister Rogers while wearing cowboy clothes. And many cities continue to air locally produced cowboy kiddie shows, which follow much the same formula hit on by Don Mahoney and Jeanna Clare.

Don and Jeanna haven't taped a new show since 1981, but they still make public appearances at supermarkets, sign autographs, wear matching western outfits, and continue to drive around in the Coupe de Ville with the top down. And even in Texas the sight of a couple of social security buckaroos barreling down the freeway sometimes merits a double take.

SEVEN

**SHARP-
SHOOTING,
TRICK
ROPING,
AND
YODELING
LOVE
SONGS**

"They're nearly naked, I'm telling you. Nearly naked! Right there on the side of the crosstown bus—N-A-K-E-D, nude women," on a subway in Manhattan a middle-aged woman rants.

"*Nearly* nude women, Mother. They are not totally unclothed," the woman's companion, her daughter, says.

"*Mostly* nude. All they wear are cowboy boots. Gladys saw their picture—*mostly naked*—ten feet tall above Times Square. *Naked! Naked cowgirls!*"

Briefly in 1991, advertisements depicting the scantily dressed cowgirl chorus line from the Broadway musical *The Will Rogers Follies* raised eyebrows in New York City. The ads also sold tickets. For the most part the pretty girls prancing across the stage in backless chaps and cowgirl G-strings delighted audiences. The show, built around the humor and rope tricks of Will Rogers, couldn't have been more all-American and even the cheesecake cowgirls seemed somehow wholesome in the flesh. Perhaps the jiggle-and-wiggle display might have been interpreted as more offensive and sexist had the women not been recreating the roles of the Ziegfeld girls who backed the cowboy star during his first New York run in 1914.

Like Buffalo Bill and Annie Oakley at Euro Disney, the Will Rogers recently roping on Broadway is portrayed by an actor. Like Bill and Annie's show in Europe, however, Will's revival proves that the world hasn't tired of cowboy and cowgirl entertainment. Just down the street from the theater where Will ropes and the nearly naked cowgirl chorus line kicks, *Cowboy Logic*—-an evening of prairie music and poetry—enjoyed a short run at the Rainbow Room atop Rockefeller Center.

Buckaroos on Broadway have long been boffo business. In *Scouts of the Plains*, Buffalo Bill starred as himself on the New York stage in 1873. The Mulhalls did their onstage rodeo in Manhattan, too. The original Will Rogers roped and joked in front of the footlights for years in the Ziegfeld Follies. And unlike the limited roles of women in western dime novels and movies and radio and TV, theatrical cowgirls had stars hanging on their dressing-room doors from the first. As Will Rogers once said, "My little old act with the lasso was just put in to kill time while girls were changing costumes."

Ethel Merman belted out the songs of Irving Berlin in the stage musical *Annie Get Your Gun*, which later became a movie starring blond bombshell Betty Hutton. Ethel put her boots on again for *Girl Crazy*, another out-West song-and-dance-fest co-starring Ginger Rogers on stage, and featuring Judy Garland and Mickey Rooney in the 1943 movie version. *Oklahoma!*, the Rodgers and Hammerstein hit of the 1940s also boasted a bevy of gingham-clad cowboys and cowgirls on stage, and later on screen.

Not that western-costumed showgirls kick up sparks only on the Great White Way. Agnes De Mille choreographed the West in her

Sincerely,
Mona Freeman

ballet *Rodeo*. Giacomo Puccini wrote an opera about it—*La Fanciulla del West* or *Girl of the Golden West*—in which all the cowpokes and forty-niners sing in Italian about poker and outlaws and whiskey drinking. And cabaret was made for cowgirl camp. Las Vegas itself is a neon western fantasy. A giant neon cowgirl beckons visitors inside Glitter Gulch Casino. At other Vegas landmarks like Westward Ho!, The Frontier, The Horseshoe, and El Rancho, a loud cowboy ambience practically slaps visitors in the face.

In California, one cowgirl cabaret act attempts to "bring a little Las Vegas" into every room they play. The Del Rubio triplets bill themselves as "three gals, three guitars, one birthday." The trio sing off key. They strum three acoustic guitars with all the precision and grace of a garden rake being dragged across a sidewalk. Their dancing? Sheesh! Terrible! The "best-if-used-by" date on their canned stage banter has long passed, too. And yet The Del Rubios' star keeps rising . . . and falling . . . and rising again.

Three bouffant hairdos—or are they wigs?—dyed canary yellow. Three sequined miniskirts with pompon tassels. Three faces made up like Bette Davis in *Whatever Happened to Baby Jane?* And six adorable white ankle-high cowgirl go-go boots. Eadie, Elena, and Millie Del Rubio just may be the last of the old-time glamour girls. Or perhaps the first of a new breed of show-business individualists.

"We have no talent," says the oldest Del Rubio sister, Millie, who was born fifteen minutes ahead of Eadie and a half hour before Elena. "Or, well . . .," she reconsiders, "we have *limited* talent. Talent

S H A R P -
S H O O T I N G ,
T R I C K
R O P I N G ,
A N D
Y O D E L I N G
L O V E
S O N G S

up to a point, let's put it that way." And yet the Del Rubios have appeared on *Late Night with David Letterman*, *Pee-Wee's Playhouse*, *Donahue*, *Married . . . with Children*, *Golden Girls*, plus a Pontiac commercial and a Diet Pepsi ad. Their first album—*Three Gals, Three Guitars*—sold well enough to merit a second, and after thirty-five off-and-on years in show business, the phone in the Del Rubios' triple-wide mobile home has finally started to ring.

The Del Rubios' secret: Be yourself no matter what. "Agents would always tell us we needed to be more like the Andrews Sisters or more like the McGuire Sisters. Then, in the 1960s, more like the Supremes," Eadie says. "Well, we thought, to heck with that. We'll just be ourselves, we decided. Do our own kind of act, and if we make a living in show business that's enough. We didn't want to be like anybody else."

None of the sisters has ever married, and each is devoted to the act. "We are courageous, and have the guts to be different," says Elena straightening her sequined skirt, "because we are never alone."

"We have courage," adds Millie, "because we are three."

The Del Rubios' song bag isn't all that country-and-western. Their act includes versions of "In-A-Gadda-Da-Vida," "Walk Like an Egyptian," and "These Boots Are Made for Walking." It's attitude more than repertoire that makes the Del Rubio sisters' cabaret seem cowgirl.

In Nashville, the singing cowgirls' repertoire sounds more traditional, leaning toward twangy tears-in-your-beer tunes. Among the first gals to sing publicly and successfully about cheatin', lyin', hard times, and heartbreak were the Carters—Sara and Maybelle—who started recording in 1927. The Carters' forte was the hillbilly sound of the southeastern United States. But in 1935, a female voice echoed in from the Southwest, when Patsy Montana recorded "I Want to Be a Cowboy's Sweetheart," the first country hit by a woman. Other cowgirl singers followed. A sister act called "The Girls of the Golden West," and another group billed as "Louise Massey & The Westerners" were among the more popular cowgirl counterparts of a whole herd of cowboy crooners. Then came Kitty Wells. Producers of the Grand Ole Opry considered Wells's hit "It Wasn't God Who Made

Honky Tonk Angels" to be too outspoken for the air waves in 1952. The number was an "answer song," which defended the women disparaged in an early Hank Thompson hit, "The Wild Side of Life."

Kitty Wells wore gingham and was packaged as the chicken-frying housewife type, but publicists painted her contemporary, Patsy Cline, as the beer-drinking, gold-lamé good-time gal. Before her death in a plane crash in 1963, Patsy recorded a string of cowgirl hits including "Crazy," "I Fall to Pieces," and "Faded Love." In the wake of Patsy Montana and Kitty Wells and Patsy Cline came Tammy Wynette, Loretta Lynn, and Dolly Parton. And now contemporary country music mixes sugary sobs and stories of heartbreak and D-I-V-O-R-C-E with loopy riffs of the pedal steel guitar. Even if the themes seem trite, the Nashville sound of the nineties is smart, literate, and sometimes topical. Baby boomers love it. Slick honky-tonk discos now pack in crowds of two-stepping MBAs along with the blue-collar regulars. Country has become the second-most-favored radio format in America behind something called adult contemporary. "Country music is soul music for white people," David Letterman's band leader, Paul Shaffer, has said, "and people always return to soul music, because that's where the heart is."

Country music stars never forget their roots. Loretta Lynn called Kitty Wells her musical mentor and credited Patsy Cline as an important influence shaping her personality. Reba McEntire covered a Patsy Cline song on each of her first three albums. Canadian torch-and-twang singer k. d. lang has even gone so far as to suggest that she is the reincarnation of Patsy Cline. She named her band the "Reclines" in a salute to her vocal idol, or perhaps to herself in her previous-life persona. Recording artist Carlene Carter hails from one of country music's most famous families; Nashville royalty so to speak, she's a descendant of Sara and May-

SHARP-
SHOOTING,
TRICK
ROPING,
AND
YODELING
LOVE
SONGS

belle, country music's first girl group. Roseanne Cash got her ear for down-home melody the genetic way too—she's the daughter of the "Man in Black," Johnny Cash. The Dixie Chicks weren't raised backstage at the Grand Ole Opry, but they harbor a healthy respect for the prairie nightingales who came before. They titled their first album "Thank Heavens for Dale Evans" as a nod to their favorite singing cowgirl.

Sitting around the henhouse in Dallas, the Dixie Chicks don't suggest any sort of cowgirl paradox. Their image mixes Dale-Evans glamour with Thelma-and-Louise grit. Television cowgirl Jeanna Clare continues to do her own thing. No man acts as the Del Rubio sisters' trail boss either. The nearly naked girls on the crosstown bus would have tickled old Calamity Jane—not so much with their exhibitionism, but with the way they shrugged off their critics and went right on with the show in such classic go-to-hell fashion.

Things seem to be looking up for cowgirls all around. Although Bonanza Jellybean, that pessimistic observer of the dreadful state of cowgirl affairs in Tom Robbins's fiction, said that the demand for cowgirls springs from the hearts of little girls. But, she continued dismally, "the reality is, we got about as much chance of growing up to be cowgirls as Eskimos have got being vegetarians." Old Bonanza Jellybean might eat her words if she met the Dixie Chicks, Sonna Warvell, Jeanna Clare, and the Del Rubios. Because of trails blazed by gals like them, salad is now being served at the igloo.

CHAPTER EIGHT

COWGIRLS CUM LAUDE

THE WORDS "cultural Mecca" and "Hereford, Texas" don't often appear in the same sentence. Come to think of it, "hotbed of intellectualism" and "Amarillo suburbs" have probably never been uttered in the same breath either. But more than a few female cowhands call the plains of the Panhandle home. Ranchers in this part of Texas, along with bordering areas of Oklahoma and New Mexico, claim responsibility for a hefty percentage of the nation's total beef production. The feedlots on the main highway make downtown Hereford smell a little like a barnyard. Cable TV comes at no extra charge with a room at the Best Western Motel. The barbecue can't be beat. The Mexican

"The Cowgirl," bronze by Shalah Perkins.

food is passable too, and five western-wear stores share enough business to stay off each other's toes. All things considered, sleepy little Hereford makes an appropriate headquarters for the world's one and only cowgirl think tank—the National Cowgirl Hall of Fame and Western Heritage Center.

In a converted ranch-style mini-mansion just off the town's main drag, seven dedicated individuals put in sixty-hour weeks cataloging cowgirl artifacts, organizing exhibitions of cowgirl culture, and collecting boxes and volumes of lore and scholarship about the women of the West. The Cowgirl Hall of Fame opened in 1975 as a receptacle and clearinghouse for all things cowgirl. With more than one hundred inductees—ranging from Lucille Mulhall to trick ropers and educators and artists and writers—the Hall of Fame pays tribute not only to the cowgirl's bravery, horsewomanship, and stylishness, but also to her philosophy, her literature, her art, and her world view.

Hall of Fame Director Margaret Formby looks every bit the cowgirl intellectual. She wears her jet black hair slicked back into a tight chignon. When she walks, her billowy skirt brushes the top of fancy cowboy boots, and pendulous silver earrings hang almost low enough to tickle her collarbone. With black-rimmed reading glasses balanced precariously on the end of her nose, Margaret's manner seems downright professorial. She speaks in a thoughtful tone with just the slightest Texas drawl about cowgirls and feminism, the psychology of rodeo, and gender roles in the Old West. When talk turns to the importance of preserving western culture, she becomes a little more animated, more intense. She removes her glasses and leans forward, stressing the importance of the Cowgirl Hall of Fame's mission. In articulating her point, Margaret Formby implies something else, something larger.

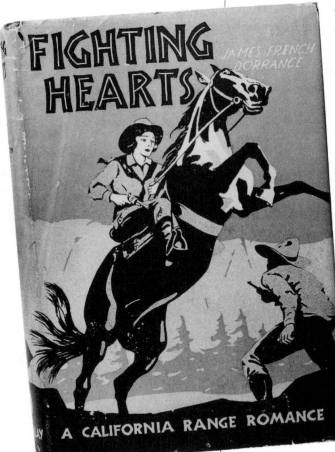

"The cowgirl is more than a pretty face, a good hand, devoted wife, and caring mother. The cowgirl is also an introspective, intellectual, creative woman," she explains, adding with a smile, "After all, a gal has plenty of time to think when sitting on the back of a horse for an eight-hour stretch or hauling cross-country to a rodeo."

The rich life of the cowgirl's mind revolves around more than horseflesh and feed prices. A woman would have to be a real mental midget to avoid at least a little bit of abstract thinking when surveying a vast western horizon at sunrise, or witnessing the birth of a calf, or galloping across open country on a sunny spring day. Imagine a

THE ROWDY GIRL'S READING LIST

Literature for Big and Little Buckaroos

- *Black Beauty*. By Anna Sewell.
- *Giant*. By Edna Ferber.
- *O Pioneers!* By Willa Cather.
- *Even Cowgirls Get the Blues*. By Tom Robbins.
- *"Dale Evans: Queen of the West"* comics.
- *Pale Horse, Pale Rider*. By Katherine Anne Porter.
- *Little House on the Prairie*. By Laura Ingalls Wilder.
- *Caddie Woodlawn*. By Carol Ryrie Brink.
- *"Annie Oakley"* comics.
- *Riders of the Purple Sage*. By Zane Grey.
- *True Grit*. By Charles Portis.
- *The Red Pony*. By John Steinbeck.
- *Hearts of the West*. By O. Henry.
- *Cowboy Dreams*. By Dayal Kaur Khalsa.
- *"Wonder Woman"* comics.
- *The Exalted One*. Poems by Sue Wallis
- *The King Ranch*. By Tom Lea.
- *My Friend Flicka*. By Mary O' Hara
- *Sidesaddle*. The Magazine of the National Cowgirl Hall of Fame.
- *Dry Crik Review*. A quarterly compendium of contemporary cowboy writing.
- *True West* magazine.
- *The Cowgirls*. By Joyce Gibson Roach.
- *Angel Unaware*. By Dale Evans.
- *Rodeo Road*. By Vera McGinnis.
- *Ten Thousand Goddam Cattle*. By Katie Lee.
- *The Cattlemen*. The monthly magazine of the National Cattlemen's Association.
- *Women's Pro Rodeo News*. The publication of the Women's Professional Rodeo Association.
- The Sheplers Catalog.
- *Cowboys Are My Weakness*. By Pam Houston.
- *Molly Ivins Can't Say That, Can She?* By Molly Ivins.
- *Cowgirls*. A coloring book by Bellerophon Books.
- *Buffalo Girls*. By Larry McMurtry.
- *The Ballad of Cat Ballou*. By Roy Chanslor.
- *Hell on Women and Horses*. By Alice Marriott.
- *The Texas Cow-Calf Management Handbook*. Texas Agricultural Extension Service.

EIGHT

COW-
GIRLS
CUM
LAUDE

Jonnie Jonckowski and friends.

moment in the life of an early working cowgirl. From her vantage point, tall in the saddle, surrounded by the awesome perfection of nature, it'd be damn difficult not to ponder the Bigger Picture every now and then.

Cowgirling in the strictest, roping-and-riding sense, leaves plenty of time for lofty contemplations. And the maverick spirit of the working cowgirl lurks within many modern women, inspiring them to tackle challenges in the arts, in politics, religion, and business. Just ask Margaret Formby and she'll tell you: "cowgirl intellectual" is not an oxymoron.

The cowgirl's inner life isn't only academic. She also has a spiritual side. When she doesn't have time to sneak into her favorite choir-loft pew at St. Pius X in Billings, bull-riding champion Lynn "Jonnie" Jonckowski improvises her own little Sunday-morning ritual—even if it happens to be a Thursday afternoon. Since she travels for weeks at a time, Jonnie sets aside a couple of predusk hours before each trip to thank "Buckwheat Up There for my gifts." She saddles her favorite horse, whistles for her dogs and trots off to a special corner of her property, "near a fox den and a marsh where some mallards live. I sit there and watch and think," she says, calling the ritual "mandatory" for her. "It's my quiet time, my church, cowgirl yoga."

Other cowgirls adhere to more rigid modes of worship. Sometimes they even shove their religious fervor onto ambivalent loved ones. Prairie homemaker Molly Goodnight taught Sunday school to her ranch's motley crew of cowboys, and forced her husband to attend church. Perhaps to please his wife, Colonel Charles Goodnight was baptized in a stock pond near Happy, Texas. A fellow ranchman later asked the Colonel which denomination he had joined. "I don't know," Colonel Goodnight replied with well-intended enthusiasm, "but it's a *damned* good one."

The majority of Americans define themselves as Christian. Cowgirls, all-American heroines, usually follow Christian doctrine, in one form or another. One cowgirl might be a fundamentalist, a fire-and-brimstone Christian who frowns upon dancing and mixed bathing, and tithes to TV preachers. The woman at the neighboring ranch, however, could espouse conservative Catholicism, while the gal down the road prays along liberal Episcopalian lines. The common thread in cowgirl theology has less to do with biblical belief than with ethics and morality. Cowgirls, almost without exception, vocally defend what politicians code "basic American values," and they strive to live by the Golden Rule—even if they don't strap on their high heels and go to Sunday school every week.

If some of us seem to connect cowgirls and cowboys with Christianity and clean living, Roy Rogers and Dale Evans might be to blame, or to bless, for that impression. A conversation with Dale Evans isn't preachy or particularly punctuated with biblical references, but Dale shares her religious views generously. She attends church regularly, her children were alumni of vacation Bible schools, and

THE COWGIRL POET

Lead Mare

By Sue Wallis

That woman there
She can be a lead mare
Has watched horses so long
And so well she can tell what goes on
In their minds

It's that high-thrown head
How she holds her shoulders
Watch ... she'll kinda hunch then
Throw her weight in ways
Unseen by us, but understood
By the saddle bunch

Once she tried it in Kentucky
That lead mare bit
And it worked there, too

At one of those fancy outfits
White board fences
Blooded thoroughbreds
She slipped away from the crowd
Stood quiet, moved her body
And they all quit grazing
Tossed her head
And they all came to her
Just like they do
At the ranch

'Course those people
Didn't notice
But she
. . . didn't care.

the Queen of the West has sung soprano with many a choir. In addition to her composition "Happy Trails to You" and other cowboy classics, Dale also writes inspirational songs.

Organizers of the Madison Square Garden Rodeo once tried to prevent Roy and Dale from including a religious number in their show. The duo discussed it and decided the issue was important, a principle worth fighting for. They took a stand, saying, "If we can't do our religious number, we won't go on at all." The New Yorkers at first balked and then conceded. A rendition of "Peace in the Valley" remained in the show. And during the following weeks Roy and Dale shattered all Madison Square Garden attendance records to date.

Dale Evans's gospel isn't just a musical message. Since the 1950s she has shared the pulpit with superstar ministers like Billy Graham. And she writes inspirational books—twenty-six of them so far. Her first and most famous literary endeavor, *Angel Unaware*, described the life and death of the Rogerses' daughter Robin, who

suffered from Down's Syndrome. The book stayed on the best-seller lists for many months and is now in its eighth printing. Today, Dale's forum is a syndicated weekly radio program called *A Date with Dale*. "I just rap with a different celebrity or notable person about current events and topics of faith," she says. "It's fun. We don't preach. That can turn off audiences." And as far as Dale Evans is concerned, the message—faith and patriotism and family—is too important to risk losing listeners.

Among cowboys and cowgirls the line between religion and patriotism gets blurry. At rodeos, big and small, flag waving and invoking blessings from above sometimes seem one and the same. The first order of rodeo business has a pretty cowgirl galloping Old Glory around the arena, as "The Star-Spangled Banner" plays and the announcer reads a few lines invariably called "The Cowboy's Prayer."

Rodeo religion doesn't end with the grand entry invocation either. As you might imagine, those men and women whose livelihoods involve straddling angry bulls have a very special relationship with God. At PRCA rodeos, most Sunday mornings feature cowboy church, where a handful of competitors will gather behind the chutes, remove their hats, and hear a word or two from the Good Book. Rodeo hands don't shy away from personal religious revelations. The cowboys and cowgirls clap, sing, stomp their feet, and eagerly share their Christian testimonies. Generally, the featured speaker at these get-togethers is a cowgirl or cowboy with another, more powerful calling than riding rough stock.

Susie Luchsinger ministers to rodeo folk. She and her husband, Paul, a former steer wrestler, call their cowboy Christian organization Psalms Ministries. "I used to sing country music," Susie says, "but the Lord called us in 1984, and he called us to work right where we were—in rodeo." Susie grew up on a ranch in Oklahoma. Her father and grandfather rode the rodeo. And her sister, Reba McEntire, started her country-music career in dusty rodeo arenas too.

Not all western women follow the most well-traveled trail to spirituality. South Texas rancher Sarita Kenedy East followed the teachings of a Trappist monk. Sarita would sit for hours in the tower

of her hacienda and meditate, usually with a little liquor to loosen her mind. Sarita died in 1961, willing part of her retreat to the Missionary Oblates of Mary Immaculate. Today, it's called Lebh Shomea, which means "listening heart" in Hebrew. The clerics maintain it as a no-talking retreat for those souls who find peace in much the same way that bull rider Jonnie Jonckowski does—through cowgirl yoga.

For many decades cowgirl art didn't hang in fancy Santa Fe galleries. And cowgirl poets weren't represented by fast-talking New York agents. These days, however, cow-country art and literature can pay as well as cattle-raising for a lucky and talented few. Why? Because the cowgirl's life and perspective have taken on mythic proportions. Everybody wants a peek at what a real-life heroine sees, a glimpse into the big heart of a genuine icon.

Traditional western art falls into two general categories: art about cowboy life created by real cowboys, and art about cowboy life as seen by outsiders. A slightly more modern category includes works by noncowboy westerners. These paintings and sculptures express the cowboy/cowgirl spirit, and present the westerner's extraordinary take on ordinary things. Whether a traditional painting of a human locked in combat with a bucking horse, or an abstract rendering of a desert flower, most western art conveys the simple idea that romanticism and realism can sometimes be the same.

Charles Marion Russell aimed at accuracy when he painted the West. Born in St. Louis, he went to Montana as a young man and worked as a cowhand there for ten years just after the Civil War. Equally skilled in several mediums—pen and ink, oils, bronze—Russell always paid special attention to detail, portraying the cowboy's world in a way some collectors believe only a true cowboy could.

Roughly the same time that Charlie Russell was tending cattle and mixing pigments in Montana Territory, Wild West shows began bringing the characters of the West to the cities of the East. Once showmen like Buffalo Bill Cody had whetted their appetites, city slickers headed West, eager to view these cowboy creatures in their natural habitats.

FILIBUSTERING AT THE OL' BOYS CLUB

A Woman's Place Is in the Dome

- Nancy Kassebaum
- Barbara Mikulski
- Barbara Boxer
- Beverly Byron
- Barbara-Rose Collins
- Cardiss Collins
- Rosa DeLauro
- Joan Kelly Horn
- Marcy Kaptur
- Barbara B. Kennelly
- Marilyn Lloyd
- Nita M. Lowey
- Jan Myers
- Patsy T. Mink
- Susan Molinari
- Constance A. Morella
- Eleanor Holmes Norton
- Mary Rose Oakar
- Elizabeth J. Patterson
- Nancy Pelosi
- Ileana Ros-Lehtinen
- Marge Roukema
- Patricia Schroeder
- Louise M. Slaughter
- Olympia J. Snowe
- Jolene Unsoeld
- Barbara Vucanovich
- Maxine Waters
- Joan Finney
- Barbara Roberts
  and

Ann Richards,
Cowgirl Governor
of Texas

Frederic Remington, a New York artist educated at Yale, was among the tourists. He visited Montana, and straightaway decided to dedicate his life to western art. Even though he continued to live in the East, Remington painted and sculpted the West. If Charles Russell was a cowboy artist, Remington was an artist who painted cowboys, specializing in the mood and emotion rather than the detailed reality of western life.

Just as the majority of early cowboys were men, so were the majority of cowboy artists. The pioneer women who took up ranch work found that after they'd put the herd to sleep, fed their husbands, and bathed their children, there was little time for sketching. Artist Georgia O'Keeffe never punched cattle, but her understanding of the southwestern landscape merited her posthumous induction into the Cowgirl Hall of Fame.

O'Keeffe was born in Wisconsin, studied art in Chicago and New York, and taught in Texas. But in the New Mexico desert, she bloomed like a wildflower. Her abstract paintings of bones, skulls, and blossoms have been hailed by critics and curators as brilliant, frank, sensitive, and sexy. Yet it's O'Keeffe's life and her philosophy, as much as her art, that qualify her as a cowgirl.

Flinty face, puckered mouth, weathered hands: even though she first headed West in the 1920s, long after the last wagon train, Georgia O'Keeffe in later life looked the part of a pioneer woman. Those who knew her say she exuded strength and softness simultaneously. She celebrated the solitude available in the desert and cared little about pleasing society at large.

O'Keeffe once declared, "I don't see why we ever think of what others think of what we do—no matter who they are—isn't it enough to express yourself? Let them all be damned—I'll do as I please."

Dallas-area painter Donna Howell-Sickles understands O'Keeffe's sentiment, and is driven by a similar philosophical motor. Donna grew up on a ranch near the Red River, but she never really considered herself a cowgirl in the working-with-animals sense. She always wears cowboy boots, however, and says she identifies with the cowgirl spirit, the independence. She views the cowgirl as every-woman, both real and unreal, a persona we have imbued with the

ROPE TRICKS AT RADCLIFFE

The Cowgirl Goes to College

In an old movie titled *Rowdy Ann*, the main character, a cattleman's daughter, is sent away to school. She carries six shooters to class, blending in among the ivory towers about like the Clampetts in Beverly Hills.

Cowboys taught New Mexico cattlewoman Linda Davis how to read. When she was just a little girl, the men working in her father's ranch crew patiently helped her learn new words by using old copies of *Ranch Romances* as a makeshift primer. Linda later graduated from the Ethel Walker School in Connecticut, and then took a degree in agricultural economics at Cornell University.

Hallie Crawford Stillwell earned a teaching certificate before marrying a rancher and ultimately choosing a career in cattle. And it was Hallie's daughter, not her two sons, who later left the ranch to pursue higher education as well. Lucille Mulhall briefly attended a posh girl's school in St. Louis. Said to be modeled after the Kleberg family of the King Ranch, the Benedicts in the novel *Giant* sent their sons to Harvard and their daughters to Wellesley. Real-life member of the King Ranch family and former U.S. Ambassador to Britain Anne Armstrong attended the Foxcroft School and graduated Phi Beta Kappa from Vassar College. Polo player and sometime cowgirl Barlee Flanders went to school at Pine Manor College and later Boston University before heading to Wyoming in search of ranch work.

At Texas Tech University in Lubbock, Fern Sawyer majored in home economics, and Cowgirl Hall of Fame Director Margaret Formby earned a double degree in English and animal husbandry. Before cowgirling in Hawaii, Alicia Neuhaus learned about advertising at the University of Texas. Vera McGinnis went to beauty college. Rebecca Gonzales got all the wisdom she felt she needed in two years at Sam Houston State. Teenage barrel racer Angie Meadors hopes to wangle a rodeo scholarship to some small college in Oklahoma. Florida rodeo hand Vana Beissinger plans to find a curriculum in animal psychology when her barrel-racing days are done.

The point? Cowgirls love learning almost as much as they love horses and cows.

When Texas rancher Electra Waggoner Biggs went East to school—first to Miss Wright's in Philadelphia and later to Columbia University in New York City—classmates teased her about being a ranch girl, poked fun at her drawl, and called her "Tex." Electra considered the drawl an asset, the nickname a compliment, and ranching an enviable heritage.

attributes of a goddess. That image forms a central theme in her art. "As women we need heroines like the cowgirl," she says. "I am using her to explore all sorts of mythological themes. I put men in my paintings sometimes too, but men already have all the heroes they need."

Not long ago, Donna made a painting of a 1920s cowgirl lounging on the back of a bull. The work was titled "Pasiphaë" after the mythical mother of the Minotaur, a half-bull half-man monster. The cowgirl can illustrate lots of legends about women, Donna has discovered. She draws inspiration from Greek and Roman myth and various world religions, sometimes portraying the cowgirl as Eve. In a painting called "The Grove," one of Donna's figures strikes a pose from an ancient East Indian sculpture. The title of another drawing, "Zeus and ERAopa," makes a sly feminist pun about the Equal Rights Amendment.

The cowgirls of Donna's world are invariably happy, smiling, exuberant. Her art carries an uplifting feminist message with a sense of humor. Donna says, "On one level the cowgirl is an accomplished and gutsy rider balanced on potential danger. On another level, she's constantly readjusting the balance of her own circumstance. As an archetype, she is a blend of past memories, present joys and future dreams."

Donna's mixed-media cowgirl canvases sell for from $650 to $7,500 in Aspen, Los Angeles, and five other cities. Celebrity collectors such as movie executive Peter Guber and actor Charlie Sheen have purchased her work. And although Donna's paintings have been dominated by cowgirls since 1971, she has witnessed a dramatic rise in buyer interest during the past two years.

"The cowgirl image," she explains, "has transcended its own reality."

Not all cowgirl artists express themselves with paints. Rancher Electra Waggoner Biggs took up sculpting when she was young primarily as a reason to convince her parents she should stay in New York City. Electra also thought she might like the feel of the clay. Much to her surprise, and everybody else's, she was good at it.

Electra wasn't just artistic; she was beautiful and glamorous. Her personal style and cowgirl panache reportedly inspired Buick to name an automobile in her honor, and Lockheed to christen a sleek new jet model "Electra" too. Electra's bridal portrait, by famed photographer Edward Steichen, appeared in Vogue in 1933. And her art had admirers as well. She mounted showings at New York galleries, ultimately selling pieces for as much as $60,000.

One of Electra's marble sculptures—"Enigma," the head of a half-black, half-Indian woman—belongs to the permanent collection of the Huntington Museum in California. She has executed bronzes of Bob Hope, Will Rogers, Harry Truman, actress Mary Martin, and other celebrities. Today, Electra is back in Texas, ranching. But she still gets her hands dirty in the studio almost daily; she still likes the feel of the clay.

EVEN COWGIRLS WRITE THE NEWS

Who, What, Where, When, and How Come

Some gals rope cattle, other cowgirls wrangle ideas.

- Connie Chung—CBS News.
- Linda Ellerbee—Syndicated columnist and commentator.
- Molly Ivins—The Fort Worth *Star-Telegram*.
- Ellen Goodman—*The Boston Globe*.
- Anna Quindlen—*The New York Times*.
- Cokie Roberts—ABC News.
- Nina Totenberg—National Public Radio.
- Barbara Walters—ABC News.

Montana artist and sometime cowgirl Carol Grende also works in bronze. She recently completed a sculpture of pioneer bronc rider Fanny Sperry Steele, and is at work on a piece depicting Annie Oakley. "From Belle to Bandit," a twelve-inch bronze by Bozeman sculptor Pamela Harr shows Belle Starr changing out of a dress into trousers. Other subjects of Harr's include Narcissa Whitman, the first white woman to cross the rockies, and Sacajawea, the Shoshoni woman who interpreted for explorers Lewis and Clark. Near Denver, Nancy Jellico sculpts in clay, then casts in bronze. Shallah Perkins sculpts and ranches in Colorado not far from the Cimarron River. Star York creates bronze cowgirl sculptures in Santa Fe.

In Washington state, Kathleen Jo Ryan cowgirls with a camera. Her photographs of ranch life are compiled in the book *Ranching Traditions*. Lea Sage snaps women's rodeo action. Texan Barney Nelson has ranched most of her life, and sometimes she carries a Nikon along in her saddlebag. Barney's photography has been exhibited in several galleries and museums and published in a volume, *Voices and Visions of the American West*.

Entire galleries and museums specialize in the art of the West. More than 350,000 pieces at the Thomas Gilcrease Museum in Tulsa tell the story of people in North America from pre-Columbian times to the present. The Buffalo Bill Historical Center exhibits western art, as does the Amon Carter Museum in Fort Worth and the Eiteljorg Museum of American Indian and Western Art in Indianapolis. In Kerrville, Texas, the Cowboy Artists of America Museum primarily shows works by contemporary male western artists. Although they don't have a museum, an organization of female painters and sculptors called the Women Artists of the West encourages and supports women artists in much the same way a cattle raisers' association lends a hand to ranchers.

Land is the cattlewoman's blank canvas. Her pigments? Cows. The cowgirl artist herds colors and shapes. And still other creative western gals wrangle words.

Each January cowgirls and cowboys descend on Elko, Nevada. No rodeo money attracts them, no cattle auction, not even the sweet

THE COWGIRL POET

Girlfriends

By Sue Wallis

In our twenties
To celebrate
We whipped men at pool
Drove a hundred miles
To a country dance
On five dollars
Easy

Now we rejoice
In faded flannel nighties
Chocolates, a bottle of wine
And old Tarzan movies
Giggling about wild times
And those men

Six-horse hitches
Bound for gay old dances
Couldn't drag us
Off these couches
De-afghan us

Handsome fellers
Lined up asking
Couldn't tempt us
From this pleasure

It's too precious
It's too rare
That's why we call it

Our indulgence

smells of a barbecue cookoff. It is love of language which lures them. Prairie literati wear boots and hats and spurs, and talk in couplets about sonnets and études and odes. At Elko's Cowboy Poetry Gathering, limericks replace rope tricks, and snazzy feats of bravery on horseback are supplanted by rhythmic feet of iambic pentameter on paper.

Roughly a third of the seventy-five or so poets have been women. Organizers say more and more cowgirl rhymers participate with each passing year. Thousands of tourists follow the poets to this corner of northeastern Nevada for three full days of readings, recitations and concerts of cowboy music. Technical workshops offer beginners tips on things such as poetry publishing and copyright laws. Open sessions give audience members a chance to read their best stuff right alongside the big-time word herders. Master cowboy poet Waddie Mitchell's way with words landed him a few chats with Johnny Carson on *The Tonight Show*. Cowgirl wordsmith Sue Wallis has waxed poetic on the tube too.

It's long been a fact of ranch life that cowboys and cowgirls tell stories. Sometimes the yarns they spin have basis in fact. Like a pearl in an oyster shell, something pretty can be created from a small grain of truth whenever cowpokes gather. But as with faux pearls, that iota of fact isn't strictly required for lustrous results. Perfectly pearly cow-camp tales can be snatched from thin air, with the teller inventing names and places and tossing in fantastic plot twists as he goes along.

In the days of the open range, cowboys relied on this fireside fiction as entertainment, escape, and sometimes as sedative. While a skilled storyteller might be recruited to take his colleagues' minds off the problems of the day, a poor talker could be counted on to bore a crew to sleep.

The gifted storyteller of the Old West developed a repertoire. He knew just how to pace his tales, how to create well-rounded characters, where to add a joke, and how to milk a suspenseful moment. In the old days, a cowboy fabulist might polish the same saga for years before he got it just right. Creators of such oral literature had ample opportunity to fine-tune their greatest hits. Every work was a work-in-progress, as favorite legends spread from campfire to campfire, territory to territory, generation to generation.

A few cowboys put pen to paper, writing their "windys" down. Charles Russell, the artist, kept a journal. In the margins, he illustrated the stories he related with little sketches of his world. J. Frank Dobie started out as a cowboy, but his talent with language surpassed his efficacy with a rope. He authored twenty books and hundreds of articles about cowboy culture, and ended up an academic, a respected professor of English at the University of Texas.

The cowboy's fictional refrains stayed mainly on the plains until the turn of the century. When the cowboy entered the eastern consciousness through Wild West shows and newspaper reports, he immediately sparked Yankee imaginations. Journalists and writers went West in hopes of inventing or encountering their own stories of cowboy adventure. When Philadelphia attorney Owen Wister published *The Virginian* in 1902, a full-blown literary genre came of age.

Melodramas on paper—the cowboy adventure stories that gained popularity during the late nineteenth and early twentieth century unfolded as morality plays set against a backdrop of teepees and cacti. Written by what one historian referred to as "pale young men from Connecticut," these dime novels represented the outsider's view

Two cowgirl poets: Jo Casteel and Tommi Jo Casteel.

of cowboy life. The stories immortalized cowboys as larger-than-life characters always fighting for virtue and honor against ridiculous odds and always triumphing just before the prairie fire reached the barn, or before the rancher's virginal daughter met a "fate worse than death" at the hands of evil savages.

Inexpensive novels published by Beadle and Adams, along with magazines such as *Rough Rider Weekly*, *Wild West Weekly*, and later *Ranch Romances* ensured that no reader went without his or her ration of western adventure. No writers of pulp fiction went hungry either. The public's appetite seemed insatiable. The fiction formula

was foolproof: Plug a different cowboy into the equation, add a fresh locale, give the villain a new name, and—presto!—there was next week's installment—unlimited cowboy adventure selling at ten cents a pop.

The first writers of cowboy literature were men. Or rather the first published were men. Some western women, however, did keep journals. While men embellished the big events of western drama, pioneer cowgirls recorded the hard facts of daily life.

Laura Ingalls Wilder's reminiscences about her youth in rugged western territory during the 1870s and 1880s evolved into a series of children's classics. Wilder's "Little House" books—*Little House on the Prairie, Little House in the Big Woods*, and others—earned her a posthumous place in the Cowgirl Hall of Fame. Novelist Willa Cather's writings about the West merited her Hall of Fame induction too. In *O Pioneers!* (1913) and other novels and short stories published during the 1920s, Cather questioned the status quo and endowed strong female protagonists with heroic characteristics earlier writers had reserved only for fictional men.

During the 1930s and 1940s, Katherine Anne Porter ran with the literary baton passed by Laura Ingalls Wilder and Willa Cather and took it to new worlds. Porter's short stories and novels allowed the western heroine to stray far from the farm. She set her fiction in New York, Mexico, and Europe, as well as her native Texas.

Porter lived briefly in Berlin during Hitler's rise. She spent time in Mexico during the revolution of 1920, worked as a newspaper reporter in Denver, and as a scriptwriter in Hollywood. Patrician and serene-looking, Porter harbored a powerful penchant for liquor and travel and men. She married four times, and tended to reinvent herself, revising her life story to suit her whims. The women of Katherine Anne Porter's fiction, like Porter herself, lived by their own rules—cowgirls without cows. "I was born free," the author once said, "and I've always stayed free."

Frank Dobie, Willa Cather, and Katherine Anne Porter write no more, but cowgirl and cowboy fiction lives on. Best-selling Larry MacMurty has had two of his westerns turned into TV mini-series. Paperback novels by Louis L'Amour fill entire shelves in bookstores.

In the tradition of *Wild West Weekly*, a monthly called *True West* continues publishing articles about cowboys, cowgirls, and life on the range. Montana-based author Tom McGuane writes movies and novels about the characters of the New West. Cowboy poets gather not only in Elko, but also in Riverton, Wyoming; Durango, Colorado; Ruidoso, New Mexico; Prescott, Arizona, and other cities to celebrate cowboy literature. Novels like Edna Ferber's *Giant* portray twentieth-

Georgie Connell Sicking, cowgirl poet.

century cowgirls as they appear to outsiders. And modern poetry, drama, and novels about courageous women fired by a cowgirl spirit thrive too.

Images of strong, competent women compel cowgirl Sue Wallis to write. Sue worked with cows for decades before she began working with words. When she was just a little girl, she and her father would drive two matched bays—one named Ulysses S. Grant, the other Robert E. Lee—when they went out to feed their cattle along Wyoming's Powder River. As they rode, Sue's dad recited from Rudyard Kipling and spoke poems by Robert Service. Sue listened. On those rides she learned about ranching and about literature.

Sue now lives in Laramie, where she attends the University of Wyoming. After finishing her degree in American Studies, she plans to pursue a master's in range management. Meanwhile, she writes. Her short stories have been featured in several journals, and her poems were recently compiled in a small volume, *The Exalted One.*

Sue says she's lately been playing around with ancient mythology in her work, much as visual artist Donna Howell-Sickles has. Sue retools old legends by setting them in ranch country. One poem, "Bríghíd," uses cowgirl colloquial language to tell the story of a Celtic goddess.

Other cowgirl writers sew

DELL JULY-SEPT. 10¢

Annie Oakley *and* **Tagg**

She dared to defy
ONE MAN'S LAW

stories from similar thread. California author-teacher Jo-Ann Mapson's collection of short fiction, *The Fault Line*, as well as her first novel, *Hank and Chloe*, feature contemporary cowboy and cowgirl characters. Although she lives in Ohio, Pam Houston wrote convincingly about cowgirl lust in *Cowboys Are My Weakness*. Still other western literature aims at younger readers. Dayal Kaur Khalsa's *Cowboy Dreams* tells of a small girl yearning to be a cowboy. Laurie Wagoner Buyer writes poems for grownups. Lisa Quinlan does poems plus extra-short short stories. Gwen Petersen couples poetry with a weekly newspaper column. And Cowgirl Hall of Famer Georgia Connell Sicking, the dean of cowgirl poets, has been ranching and rhyming for more than a half century.

John Dofflemyer ranches in California and publishes a literary quarterly, *The Dry Crik Review*, devoted to serious cowboy and cowgirl writing. He's been catching some flak from cowboys lately for filling issues with the work of too many women writers. "I'm not consciously trying to publish more women," he says, "but they're the ones sending me powerful poems and stories. They seem to have something important to say."

In Tom Robbins's novel *Even Cowgirls Get the Blues*, a character named Bonanza Jellybean said a mouthful when she pointed out: "Cowgirls exist as an image. A fairly common image. The *idea* of cowgirls prevails in our culture. Therefore, it seems to me, the *fact* of cowgirls should prevail."

For some cowgirls it's a short journey from the pastures of the prairie to the groves of academe. Joyce Gibson Roach grew up surrounded by ranching culture in Jack County, Texas. Today, she's a cowgirl academic, an author and adjunct instructor of southwestern literature at Texas Christian University in Fort Worth. She has won critical praise for her

two musical plays about western women. She writes short stories on topics such as barrel racing and Brahman bulls. One of her books, *The Cowgirls*, earned the Western Writers of America's Spur Award for best western non-fiction. Through her writings and lectures, Roach has come to be recognized as the a premier expert on cowgirls and their role in the Old West as well as in contemporary pop culture.

She speaks articulately about historic and modern-day cowgirls as a specific group of working women. She studies how and why today's women, through fashion and show business, choose to imitate the cowgirl's life. But Roach is also fascinated by the idea of the cowgirl as a character of myth.

Does the cowgirl represent sort of a fantasy alter ego for American women? Is she an ideal we've created? An idol we can strive to emulate, but never actually be?

Roach says: "I'm inclined to believe that the Women's Movement didn't begin with Susan B. Anthony and all those suffragettes. It began when a ranch woman first got on a good cow horse. Pioneer ranch women differed from farm women, you see. The farmer's view was ground level, usually behind a plow, where the rump of a mule dimmed her perspective. But when the ranch woman climbed atop a horse, new vistas opened up. The perspective was different. From the saddle she could see the horizon. The view inspired confidence and competence and courage. Today the cowgirl has become an elusive figure, always moving away, riding off into the sunset. We get only a glimpse of her, but a glimpse is enough. We see her outline and each fill in the details for ourselves."

"Cowgirl," insists Joyce Gibson Roach, "is a condition of the heart."

PHOTO CREDITS

CHAPTER 1

p. 3, Cow Girl with Buffalo Bill's Wild West, from *Box-Office Buckaroos: The Cowboy Hero from the Wild West Show to the Silver Screen*, by Robert Heide and John Gilman, Abbeville Publishing Group: New York. Reprinted by written permission of Robert Heide and John Gilman.

p. 4, Lucille Mulhall, from the archives of the National Cowgirl Hall of Fame and Western Heritage Center in Hereford, Texas. Reprinted by written permission of the National Cowgirl Hall of Fame and Western Heritage Center.

p.11, Cowgirl trading card, from *Box-Office Buckaroos: The Cowboy Hero from the Wild West Show to the Silver Screen*, by Robert Heide and John Gilman, Abbeville Publishing Group: New York. Reprinted by written permission of Robert Heide and John Gilman.

p. 13, Trigger and Buttermilk, reprinted by written permission of The Roy Rogers/Dale Evans Museum, Victorville, California.

p. 17, Pioneer rodeo gals of the 1920s, from the Archives of the Buffalo Bill Historical Center, Cody, Wyoming. Reprinted by written permission of the Buffalo Bill Historical Center.

p. 21, from "Dale Evans Queen of the West Comics," reprinted by written permission of The Roy Rogers/Dale Evans Museum, Victorville, California.

p. 22, Vintage cowboy/cowgirl knickknacks, from *Box-Office Buckaroos: The Cowboy Hero from the Wild West Show to the Silver Screen*, by Robert Heide and John Gilman, Abbeville Publishing Group: New York. Reprinted by written permission of Robert Heide and John Gilman.

CHAPTER 2

p. 23, A daughter of the Wild West, from *Box-Office Buckaroos: The Cowboy Hero from the Wild West Show to the Silver Screen*, by Robert Heide and John Gilman, Abbeville Publishing Group: New York. Reprinted by written permission of Robert Heide and John Gilman.

p. 25, Six Justin boots from the 1992 collection, reprinted by written permission of the Justin Boot Company.

p. 31, Four cowboy hats, reprinted by written permission of T. J. Jordan & Associates for Resistol/Stetson.

p. 34, Cowgirl trading cards, from *Box-Office Buckaroos: The Cowboy Hero from the Wild West Show to the Silver Screen*, by Robert Heide and John Gilman, Abbeville Publishing Group: New York. Reprinted by written permission of Robert Heide and John Gilman.

p. 38, Rodeo belt buckle, courtesy Gist Custom & Trophy Buckles. Reprinted by written permission of Gist, Inc.

p. 39, from "Dale Evans Queen of the West Comics," reprinted by written permission of The Roy Rogers/Dale Evans Museum, Victorville, California.

p. 40, Nancy Kelley Sheppard with lasso, reprinted by written permission of Nancy Kelley Sheppard.

CHAPTER 3

p. 43, Cowboy in Coma, vintage postcard from the Ken Brown Collection.

p. 44, Chuck wagon breakfast, courtesy Toni Frissell Collection, Library of Congress, and King Ranch Archives. Reprinted by written permission of the King Ranch Archives.

p. 48, Mobile home illustration by Karla Roberson Puckett, printed by written permission of Karla Roberson Puckett.

pp. 49–50, Ranchette illustration by Karla Roberson Puckett, printed by written permission of Karla Roberson Puckett.

p. 52, Cowgirl trading card, from *Box-Office Buckaroos: The Cowboy Hero from the Wild West Show to the Silver Screen*, by Robert Heide and John Gilman, Abbeville Publishing Group: New York. Reprinted by written permission of Robert Heide and John Gilman.

p. 53, Big House at the King Ranch, courtesy Toni Frissell Collection, Library of Congress, and King Ranch Archives. Reprinted by written permission of the King Ranch Archives.

p. 54, Cowboy interior, photo by Don A. Hoffman. Reprinted by written permission of Deep Texas, Houston.

p. 55, Beefmaster Chair by Cathy Boswell, reprinted by written permission of Cathy Boswell.

p. 55, Longhorn fabric by Guadalupe Hand Prints, Inc., San Antonio. Reprinted by written permission of McAllister Design Associates, Inc., dba Guadalupe Hand Prints, Inc.

p. 55, Cowboy dinnerware by Till Goodan, reprinted by written permission of Betty Goodan Andrews.

p. 61, from "Dale Evans Queen of the West Comics," reprinted by written permission of The Roy Rogers/Dale Evans Museum, Victorville, California.

CHAPTER 4

p. 63, Cowboy valentine, from *Box-Office Buckaroos: The Cowboy Hero from the Wild West Show to the Silver Screen*, by Robert Heide and John Gilman, Abbeville Publishing Group: New York. Reprinted by written permission of Robert Heide and John Gilman.

p. 66, Cowgirl bride, photo by Machel Elam. Reprinted by written permission of Machel Elam.

p. 69, Tad Lucas with daughter Mitzi in hat, from the archives of the National Cowgirl Hall of Fame and Western Heritage Center in Hereford, Texas. Reprinted by written permission of the National Cowgirl Hall of Fame and Western Heritage Center.

p. 74, Wedding on horseback, from the archives of the National Cowgirl Hall of Fame and Western Heritage Center in Hereford, Texas. Reprinted by written permission of the National Cowgirl Hall of Fame and Western Heritage Center.

p. 76, Dance steps illustration by Karla Roberson Puckett, printed by written permission of Karla Roberson Puckett.

p. 78, from "Dale Evans Queen of the West Comics," reprinted by written permission of The Roy Rogers/Dale Evans Museum, Victorville, California.

CHAPTER 5

p. 85, Seductive cowgirl, from *Box-Office Buckaroos: The Cowboy Hero from the Wild West Show to the Silver Screen*, by Robert Heide and John Gilman, Abbeville Publishing Group: New York. Reprinted by written permission of Robert Heide and John Gilman.

p. 89, Bull-riding cowgirl, photo by Lea Sage. Reprinted by written permission of Lea Sage.

p. 90, Nancy Binford cartoon, 1950. Previously published by the National Cowgirl Hall of Fame and Western Heritage Center in Hereford, Texas. Reprinted by written permission of Nancy Binford.

pp. 92–93, Team roping, photo by Lea Sage. Reprinted by written permission of Lea Sage.

p. 99, Christina Sanchez, bullfighter. Photo by Diego Goldberg/ SYGMA. Reprinted by written permission of SYGMA.

p. 101, Little goat roper, reprinted by written permission of the National Little Britches Rodeo Association.

p. 102, Rope trick illustration by Karla Roberson Puckett, printed by written permission of Karla Roberson Puckett.

p. 105, from "Dale Evans Queen of the West Comics," reprinted by written permission of The Roy Rogers/Dale Evans Museum, Victorville, California.

p. 107, Cowgirl trading card, from *Box-Office Buckaroos: The Cowboy Hero from the Wild West Show to the Silver Screen*, by Robert Heide and John Gilman, Abbeville Publishing Group: New York. Reprinted by written permission of Robert Heide and John Gilman.

CHAPTER 6

p. 109, Cowgirl in chaps with rope, from the Archives of the Buffalo Bill Historical Center, Cody, Wyoming. Reprinted by written permission of the Buffalo Bill Historical Center.

p. 110, "Why I Want to Be a Cowgirl," by Blaire Bresnan. Printed by written permission of Julie and Blaire Bresnan.

pp. 112–113, Brand illustrations by Karla Roberson Puckett, printed by written permission of Karla Roberson Puckett.

p. 117, Helen Campbell Kleberg, courtesy Toni Frissell Collection, Library of Congress, and King Ranch Archives. Reprinted by written permission of the King Ranch Archives.

p. 120, Cow illustration by Karla Roberson Puckett, printed by written permission of Karla Roberson Puckett.

p. 126, Cowboy/cowgirl sand pails, from *Box-Office Buckaroos: The Cowboy Hero from the Wild West Show to the Silver Screen*, by Robert Heide and John Gilman, Abbeville Publishing Group: New York. Reprinted by written permission of Robert Heide and John Gilman.

p. 127, from "Dale Evans Queen of the West Comics," reprinted by written permission of The Roy Rogers/Dale Evans Museum, Victorville, California.

CHAPTER 7

p. 129, Roy Rogers and Dale Evans with Trigger, reprinted by written permission of The Roy Rogers/Dale Evans Museum, Victorville, California.

p. 130, The Dixie Chicks, photo by Carolyn McGovern. Reprinted by written permission of The Dixie Chicks.

p. 133, Sonna Warvell as Annie Oakley, printed by written permission of Sonna Warvell.

p. 135, Cowgirl and Coke, courtesy of the Coca-Cola Company. Reprinted by written permission of the Coca-Cola Company.

pp. 140–141, Cowgirl stamps, from the Archives of the Buffalo Bill Historical Center, Cody, Wyoming. Reprinted by written permission of the Buffalo Bill Historical Center.

p. 142, Nancy Kelley Sheppard on horseback, reprinted by written permission of Nancy Kelley Sheppard.

p. 145, Don Mahoney and Jeanna Clare with Kiddie Troopers, reprinted by written permission of Jeanna Clare.

p. 147, Gene Autry, Patsy Montana, and June Storey, reprinted by written permission of Patsy Montana.

p. 150, from "Dale Evans Queen of the West Comics," reprinted by written permission of The Roy Rogers/Dale Evans Museum, Victorville, California.

p. 153, Cowgirl trading card, from *Box-Office Buckaroos: The Cowboy Hero from the Wild West Show to the Silver Screen*, by Robert Heide and John Gilman, Abbeville Publishing Group: New York. Reprinted by written permission of Robert Heide and John Gilman.

CHAPTER 8

p. 157, "The Cowgirl," by Shalah Perkins, printed by written permission of Shalah Perkins.

p. 158, Fighting Hearts, from *Box-Office Buckaroos: The Cowboy Hero from the Wild West Show to the Silver Screen*, by Robert Heide and John Gilman, Abbeville Publishing Group: New York. Reprinted by written permission of Robert Heide and John Gilman.

p. 160, Lynn "Jonnie" Jonckowski, photo by Melanie Stevens. Reprinted by written permission of Lynn Jonckowski.

p. 162, from "Dale Evans Queen of the West Comics," reprinted by written permission of The Roy Rogers/Dale Evans Museum, Victorville, California.

p. 165, Ann Richards, courtesy of Governor Ann Richards's Office. Printed by written permission of Governor Ann Richards's Office.

p. 168, *Cosmopolitan* magazine cover, from *Box-Office Buckaroos: The Cowboy Hero from the Wild West Show to the Silver Screen*, by Robert Heide and John Gilman, Abbeville Publishing Group: New York. Reprinted by written permission of Robert Heide and John Gilman.

p. 172, *Lariat* magazine cover, from *Box-Office Buckaroos: The Cowboy Hero from the Wild West Show to the Silver Screen*, by Robert Heide and John Gilman, Abbeville Publishing Group: New York. Reprinted by written permission of Robert Heide and John Gilman.

p. 173, Two cowgirl poets, photo by Sheila Dunn. Reprinted by written permission of Sheila Dunn.

p. 175, Georgie Connell Sicking, photo by S. R. Hinrichs. Reprinted by written permission of Western Folklife Center, Elko, Nevada.

p. 176, Cover from "Annie Oakley and Tagg" comics previously published by Dell Publishing, Inc.

p. 177, Cowgirl trading card, from *Box-Office Buckaroos: The Cowboy Hero from the Wild West Show to the Silver Screen*, by Robert Heide and John Gilman, Abbeville Publishing Group: New York. Reprinted by written permission of Robert Heide and John Gilman.

p. 178, Cowgirl trading card, from *Box-Office Buckaroos: The Cowboy Hero from the Wild West Show to the Silver Screen*, by Robert Heide and John Gilman, Abbeville Publishing Group: New York. Reprinted by written permission of Robert Heide and John Gilman.